FRANCIS HUTCHESON:
AN INQUIRY CONCERNING BEAUTY, ORDER,
HARMONY, DESIGN

ARCHIVES INTERNATIONALES D'HISTOIRE DES IDEES

INTERNATIONAL ARCHIVES OF THE HISTORY OF IDEAS

*Series Minor*

9

PETER KIVY

# FRANCIS HUTCHESON: AN INQUIRY CONCERNING BEAUTY, ORDER, HARMONY, DESIGN

# FRANCIS HUTCHESON: AN INQUIRY CONCERNING BEAUTY, ORDER, HARMONY, DESIGN

EDITED, WITH AN INTRODUCTION AND NOTES

*by*

PETER KIVY

MARTINUS NIJHOFF / THE HAGUE / 1973

ISBN 90 247 1545 8

# CONTENTS

# NOTE ON THE TEXT

Until very recently Francis Hutcheson was considered important merely as an "historical" figure in the history of philosophy: a "predecessor" of Hume in morals, and an "early" practitioner of philosophical aesthetics whose speculations on this regard could be passed over with a polite and knowing nod. The view that Hutcheson was not a first-rate moral theorist in his own right can no longer be sustained; and a reevaluation of Hutcheson as aesthetician seems to be called for as well. Towards such a reevaluation, Hutcheson's small but highly significant corpus of writings on aesthetics and criticism is offered here in a modern scholarly edition – the first since the eighteenth century.

Ethics was Hutcheson's overriding philosophical concern; and he continued to write about it until the time of his death. But aesthetics, although central to his thinking, was written upon once and for all – in 1725, the year of his first major publications. The entire aesthetic output, except for passing remarks in the later ethical writings, is contained in the *Inquiry Concerning Beauty, Order, Harmony, Design*, and three essays on laughter which have been here included in an appendix.

The *Inquiry Concerning Beauty, Order, Harmony, Design* is the first of two treatises which together comprise Hutcheson's first major work, the *Inquiry into the Original of Our Ideas of Beauty and Virtue*. It went through four editions during the author's lifetime: the first in 1725, the second in 1726, the third in 1729, the fourth in 1738, all under his supervision. There has been no complete modern edition of either treatise, although the second edition of the second treatise was reprinted almost entire in Selby-Bigge's *British Moralists*, and a facsimile of the fourth edition of both treatises was published recently.

Hutcheson made considerable alterations in the second, third, and fourth editions of the *Inquiry*, some of genuine philosophical interest. The present version of the first treatise follows the text of the fourth edition. It has, however, been collated with the first, second, and third (for the first time). Passages which have alternate readings in earlier editions are in square brackets in the text; the alternate readings are in the numbered notes to these bracketed passages. Many changes are minor ones; but it was thought that the decision as to what is minor and what is not should be left to the reader rather than the editor: therefore, *all* changes, except those in spelling, punctuation, capitalization, and italics, have been indicated. Spelling, punctuation, capitalization, and italics, have, for the most part, been regularized in accordance with modern usage. Most abbreviations have been spelled out. In the rare instances in which a passage enclosed in square brackets has further alternate readings, parentheses are used and the alternate readings given in the numbered notes to these passages. Footnotes in the text, indicated by asterisks, are Hutcheson's; all numbered notes are the editor's. The marginal headings are Hutcheson's, and were added in the second edition.

In 1725, the same year which saw publication of the *Inquiry Concerning Beauty, Order, Harmony, Design*, Hutcheson published six "letters" in the *Dublin Journal*. They were later reprinted by the editor of the *Dublin Journal*, James Arbuckle, in *A Collection of Letters and Essays on Several Subjects, Lately Published in the Dublin Journal* (London, 1729), which collection was reprinted again in 1734. Finally, they were collected in a separate volume under the title *Reflections Upon Laughter, and Remarks Upon "The Fable of the Bees"* (Glasgow, 1750). The first three of these papers, dated Saturday, June 5, 1725, Saturday, June 12, 1725, and Saturday, June 19, 1725, which comprise the *Reflections Upon Laughter*, are presented here in the text of the last-mentioned edition. There do not seem to have been any changes of substance in any of the editions. All notes indicated by asterisks are Hutcheson's; all numbered notes are the editor's. The spelling, punctuation, capitalization, and italics have, for the most part, been regularized in accordance with modern usage; and most of the abbreviations have been spelled out fully.

# AN
# INQUIRY

INTO THE

## ORIGINAL of our IDEAS

O F

# *BEAUTY* and *VIRTUE*;

## In Two TREATISES.

IN WHICH

The Principles of the late Earl of SHAFTSBURY are explain'd and defended, againſt the Author of the *Fable of the Bees*:

AND THE

Ideas of *Moral Good* and *Evil* are eſtabliſh'd, according to the Sentiments of the antient *Moraliſts*.

With an Attempt to introduce a *Mathematical Calculation* in Subjeſts of *Morality*.

---

Itaque eorum ipſorum quæ aſpeſtu ſentiuntur, nullum aliud animal pulchritudinem, venuſtatem, convenientiam partium ſentit : Quam ſimilitudinem natura ratioque ab oculis ad animum transferens, multo etiam magis pulchritudinem, conſtantiam, ordinem in conſiliis, faſtiſque conſervandum putat : Quibus ex rebus conflatur & efficitur id quod quærimus honeſtum : Quod etiamſi nobilitatum non ſit, tamen honeſtum ſit : quodque etiamſi à nullo laudetur, naturâ eſt laudabile. Formam quidem ipſam & faciem honeſti vides, quæ ſi oculis cerneretur, mirabiles amores excitaret ſapientiæ. *Cic. de Off. lib.* 1. *c.* 4.

---

## *LONDON*:

Printed by J. DARBY in *Bartholomew-Cloſe*, for W IL. and JOHN SMITH on the *Blind Key* in *Dublin* ; and ſold by W. and J. INNYS at the Weſt-End of St. *Paul's* Churchyard, J. OSBORN and T. LONGMAN in *Pater-Noſter-Row*, and S. CHANDLER in the *Poultry*. M. DCC. XXV.

And so no other animal has a sense of beauty, loveliness, harmony in the visible world; and Nature and Reason, extending the analogy of this from the world of

4

sense to the world of spirit, find that beauty, consistency, order are far more to be maintained in thought and deed. . . . It is from these elements that is forged and fashioned that moral goodness which is the subject of this inquiry – something that, even though it be not generally ennobled, is still worthy of all honour; and by its own nature, we correctly maintain, it merits praise, even though it be praised by none. . . . You see here . . . the very form and as it were the face of Moral Goodness; "and if," as Plato says, "it could be seen with the physical eye, it would awaken a marvelous love of wisdom." Trans. Walter Miller.

# EDITOR'S INTRODUCTION

## THE SENSE OF BEAUTY: A FIRST APPROXIMATION

It is generally acknowledged that during the first half of the eighteenth century a profound change was wrought in the theory of art and natural beauty. To this period we owe the establishment of the modern system of the arts.[1] In England, the notion of a separate and autonomous discipline devoted solely to art and to beauty came into being through the concept of "aesthetic disinterestedness."[2] In addition, emphasis in the theory of art shifted from object to subject – from the work of art to the perceiver and critic. Focal point for this change was the sense of beauty which, in concert with the moral sense of the British school, represented a dominant force in Enlightenment value theory. It is Francis Hutcheson who, more than anyone else, can be thought of as the founder and principal spokesman of this philosophical coterie.

If the aesthetic sense was instrumental in the transfer of interest, in the philosophy of art, from object to perceiver, the aesthetic and moral senses together were no less important in a parallel transference of value judgment from the rational to the sensate. Kant recognized this when he wrote, in 1762, with obvious reference to Hutcheson and the British moral sense school, "it is only in our own day that we first began to realize that the capacity of perceiving the *true* is knowledge, whereas that of sensing the *good* is *feeling*, and that the two must, under no circumstances be confused."[3] Reading "beautiful" for "good" here we

[1] See Paul O. Kristeller, "The Modern System of the Arts (II)," *Journal of the History of Ideas*, XIII (1952).

[2] See Jerome Stolnitz, "On the Origins of 'Aesthetic Disinterestedness,' " *Journal of Aesthetics and Art Criticism*, XX (1961).

[3] Quoted in Paul Arthur Schilpp, *Kant's Pre-Critical Ethics* (2nd ed.; Evanston: Northwestern University Press, 1960), p. 31. Kant, of course, later rejected the "moral sense" and the ethics of sentiment in his mature ethical writings.

have an accurate characterization of this profound change in the theory of aesthetics which Hutcheson had such a major role in effecting.

It is easy – perhaps a little too easy – to state Hutcheson's theory of the aesthetic sense. Beneath such easy statements lies a region of vagueness that has not been carefully explored heretofore. Before we turn to this more careful exploration, though, I want, in this section and the one following, to present Hutcheson's aesthetics in broad outline, in order to get a view of the gross organism.

In a definition that has often been quoted, Hutcheson gives us the basic premise of his aesthetic theory: "the word *beauty* is taken for the *idea raised in us,* and a *sense* of beauty for *our power of receiving this idea."* [4] One might say that Hutcheson had made manifest here a position towards which aesthetics and criticism had been gravitating for the preceding fifty years; it is all summed up in that succinct (and deceptively simple) phrase *"beauty* is taken for *the idea raised in us."* Many had said it implicitly: it remained for Hutcheson to say it, and mean it, and try to deal with the philosophical consequences of the position.

But if beauty "is" an idea, it is an idea occasioned, nonetheless, by an objective quality of the world – a quality of "external" objects. "Since it is certain," writes Hutcheson, "that we have *ideas* of beauty and harmony, let us examine what *quality* in objects excites these ideas, or is the occasion of them." [5] The conclusion of Hutcheson's examination is that "The figures which excite in us the ideas of beauty seem to be those in which there is *uniformity amidst variety."* [6] That, in a word, is Hutcheson's theory of beauty – but, we must hasten to add, only his theory of *absolute* or *original* beauty: "that beauty which we perceive in objects without comparison to any thing external. . . ." There is, however, another kind, *relative* or *comparative* beauty: "that which we perceive in objects commonly considered as *imitations* or *resemblances* of something else." [7]

Absolute beauty, for Hutcheson, occupies a realm of pure form: a realm that includes visible and aural forms, man-made or natural, animate or inanimate; and intelligible forms as embodied in the constructs of scientific theories. A form – be it a geometrical figure, a celestial phenomenon, a plant or animal, a theorem in physics – occasions the idea of beauty to the extent that it possesses *unity amidst variety.* By

[4] Francis Hutcheson, *An Inquiry Concerning Beauty, Order, Harmony, Design,* Section I, Article IX. Text of present edition.
[5] *Ibid.,* Section II, Article I.
[6] *Ibid.,* Section II, Article III.
[7] *Ibid.,* Section I, Article XVI.

far the largest and most widely appreciated class of such forms is that of natural beauties: "In every part of the world which we call beautiful there is a surprising uniformity amidst an almost infinite variety." [8] But for those capable of theoretical understanding, mathematics, the natural sciences, and metaphysics offer too the *unity amidst variety* that is beauty's prerequisite. "For in one theorem [unity] we may find included, with the most exact agreement, an infinite multitude of particular truths [variety]. . . ." [9] And art, though its major effects are due to comparative beauty and, as we shall see, moral content, can claim a share in the absolute beauty of form. "As to the works of art, were we to run through the various artificial contrivances or structures, we should constantly find the foundation of the beauty which appears in them to be some kind of uniformity or unity of proportion among the parts, and of each part to the whole." [10] Music, of course, is the art freest of representation and, therefore, the art *par excellence* of absolute beauty.

Under *original beauty* we may include *harmony*, or *beauty of sound*, if that expression can be allowed, because harmony is not usually conceived as an imitation of anything else. Harmony often raises pleasure in those who know not what is the occasion of it; and yet the foundation of this pleasure is known to be a sort of uniformity.[11]

But art, as we said, owes its major effects to relative beauty and to morality; to these we must now turn.

"All beauty," writes Hutcheson, "is relative to the sense of some mind perceiving it; but what we call *relative* is that which is apprehended in any object commonly considered as an *imitation* of some original. And this beauty," he continues, "is founded on a conformity, or a kind of unity between the original and the copy." [12] The beauty of imitation covers, for Hutcheson, the whole spectrum of art. That it is the basis of the visual arts goes without saying. That it is also the basis of the literary arts is hardly more surprising: "this relative beauty is what they [the poets] should principally endeavour to obtain, as the peculiar beauty of their works." [13] The same may be said for music (although to a far lesser degree): music too has its mimetic part. The tradition of emotive mimesis, with its roots in Plato and Aristotle, endured throughout most of the Enlightenment, particularly in Germany and England, reexpressed

---

[8] *Ibid.*, Section II, Article V.
[9] *Ibid.*, Section III, Article II.
[10] *Ibid.*, Section III, Article VII.
[11] *Ibid.*, Section II, Article XIII.
[12] *Ibid.*, Section IV, Article I.
[13] *Ibid.*, Section IV, Article II.

in the Doctrine of the Affections (*Affektenlehre*). Hutcheson writes:

There is also another charm in music to various persons, which is distinct from harmony and is occasioned by its raising agreeable passions. The human voice is obviously varied by all the stronger passions: now when our ear discerns any resemblance between the air of a tune, whether sung or played upon an instrument, either in its time, or modulation, or any other circumstance, to the sound of the human voice in any passion, we shall be touched by it in a very sensible manner, and have melancholy, joy, gravity, thoughtfulness excited in us by a sort of *sympathy* or *contagion*.[14]

Relative beauty is occasioned through a *relation* only; thus the absolute beauty of the object imitated is not a necessary condition: "to obtain comparative beauty alone, it is not necessary that there be any beauty in the original," writes Hutcheson; "The imitation of absolute beauty may indeed in the whole make a more lovely piece, and yet an exact imitation shall still be beautiful, though the original were entirely void of it." [15] But there is another kind of beauty besides the absolute which an object of imitation may possess. Hutcheson thought of beauty not merely as an aesthetic category; it was for him a moral category too. And he believed that the most proper objects of artistic representation are moral objects. Thus we must seek out Hutcheson the moralist to complete his philosophy of art.

The ethical theory parallels the aesthetic; it begins with the identification of moral value with an idea: "The word *moral goodness* ... denotes our idea of some quality apprehended in actions, which procures approbation, attended with desire of the agent's happiness." [16] The parallel continues: the idea of moral goodness is associated with a *moral sense* which "has this in common with our other senses, that however our desire of virtue may be counterbalanced by interest, our sentiment or perception of its beauty cannot...." [17] The moral sense, like the five bodily senses, is not subject to the will: we cannot will not to see, if our eyes are open and there is light to see.

The contribution of the moral sense to artistic appreciation, particularly in literature, is considerable, according to Hutcheson.

We shall find this sense to be the foundation also of the chief pleasures of poetry. We hinted, in the former Treatise, at the foundation of delight in numbers, measures, metaphors, similitudes. But as the contemplation of moral objects, either of

---

[14] *Ibid.*, Section VI, Article XII.
[15] *Ibid.*, Section IV, Article I.
[16] Francis Hutcheson, *An Inquiry Concerning Moral Good and Evil*, Section I, Article I. Text of 4th ed., with spelling modernized and some italics removed.
[17] *Ibid.*, Section I, Article V.

vice or virtue, affects us more strongly, and moves our passions in a quite different and more powerful manner than natural beauty, or (what we commonly call) deformity, so the most moving beauties bear a relation to our moral sense, and affect us more vehemently than the representations of natural objects in the liveliest descriptions. Dramatic and epic poetry are entirely addressed to this sense, and raise our passions by the fortunes of character, distinctly represented as morally good or evil. . . .[18]

On the one hand, one would think that Hutcheson wishes to attribute some pleasure in art to the agreeable feelings that arise when the moral sense contemplates the representation of moral excellence. Now "Moral evil," Hutcheson tells us, ". . . excites aversion and dislike." [19] Thus, if the moral sense *qua* moral sense experiences pleasure in the contemplation of moral beauty in art, it should, upon contemplation of evil and vice, experience "aversion and dislike." But it is clear that the artist cannot be limited to the representation of moral beauty; we must, after all, have our Iagos and Clytaemnestras. And even if, in the end, the good prosper and the evil suffer ("That is what fiction means," Miss Prism remarks), the moral sense nevertheless is left, in the middle, with objects of aversion and dislike. Here, a second tradition, that of emotive arousal, enters the picture. For moral qualities, both the good and the bad, "raise our passions" – an aesthetic goal universally acknowledged in Hutcheson's day, but a goal distinct from that of gratifying the moral sense through the presence of moral beauty.

It should be noted that relative beauty too plays a role in rendering the depiction of vice pleasurable. For, Hutcheson argues, as pleasing as morally perfect literary characters might be in themselves, they could hardly be said to reflect faithfully the morally imperfect world of men and affairs. Thus we take from Peter and give to Paul. The depiction of the morally vicious may deprive the moral sense of a pleasure, but it pays a return to the aesthetic sense in the form of realism: imitative beauty. Hutcheson writes:

a poet should not draw his characters perfectly virtuous. These characters indeed abstractly considered might give more pleasure, and have more beauty than the imperfect ones which occur in life with a mixture of good and evil; but it may suffice at present to suggest against this choice that we have more lively ideas of imperfect men with all their passions, than of morally perfect heroes such as really never occur to our observation, and of which consequently we cannot judge exactly as to their agreement with the copy.[20]

[18] *Ibid.*, Section VI, Article VII.
[19] *Ibid.*, Section I, Article I.
[20] *Ibid.*, Section IV, Article II. Hutcheson recognizes, in *An Essay on the Nature and Conduct of the Passions and Affections* (London, 1728), a secondary pleasure

Hutcheson's *Inquiry*, as a whole, gives intimation of wider vistas than are to be seen in the traditional notion of "moral lessons." [21] The contemplation of moral beauty in art gives rise to pleasures of sense, both aesthetic and moral; and these pleasures are ends in themselves. Yet they are ends that, one feels, cannot but deepen our moral nature and, in a more meaningful sense than didactic art, contribute to the moral progress of mankind. There is suggestion here of what is to come in German philosophy and, for me at least, a glimmering of Shelley's feeling for the ethical calling of the artist. "Didactic poetry is my abhorrence . . . ," Shelley wrote; "My purpose has hitherto been simply to familiarize the highly refined imagination of the more select classes of poetical readers with beautiful idealisms of moral excellence; aware that until the mind can love, and admire, and trust, and hope, and endure, reasoned principles of moral conduct are seeds cast upon the highway of life which the unconscious passenger tramples into dust, although they would bear the harvest of happiness." [22] I think Hutcheson has gone some way towards the appreciation of sentiments such as these.

### THE SENSE OF BEAUTY AND THE STANDARD OF TASTE

The question of the "standard of taste" is the *idée fixe* of Enlightenment aesthetic theory. The growing appeal to subjective rather than objective criteria in aesthetic judgment naturally led to the fear that a notion of "correct" and "incorrect" judgment, of "good" taste and "bad," could not be philosophically sustained. For the Enlightenment, the answer to the question of a subjective standard of taste was an abiding faith in an unchanging *human nature*. The eighteenth-century quest in aesthetics was true to the earliest vision in Western philosophy: permanence in a world of apparent flux. And Kant was spokesman for his age when he wrote with regard to the beautiful, "We are suitors for

arising from the contemplation of evil: "When the idea is . . . formed of any morally evil action, . . . there arises reluctance, or aversion. If we have committed such a crime, upon like reflection we feel the sorrow called remorse. If we have resisted the temptation, we feel a secret joy and self-approbation . . ." (pp. 69-70, spelling and punctuation modernized, and italics removed). That this is the result partly of "reflection" indicates that it is of a different nature from the immediate flush of pleasure that the moral sense feels in contemplation of the good.

[21] Hutcheson wrote, in the *Essay on the Nature and Conduct of the Passions and Affections*, "When we form the idea of a morally good action, or see it represented in the drama, or read it in epics or romance, we feel a desire arising of doing the like" (p. 69).

[22] Preface to *Prometheus Unbound*.

agreement from everyone else, because we are fortified with a ground common to all." [23] The common ground is human nature, its aesthetic expression the sense of beauty.

If an aesthetician claims, as Hutcheson did, that we have a common basis for our predilections, his first gambit is usually to minimize the prima facie differences. This Hutcheson attempted; he did so by claiming that although differences exist, many do not concern the bedrock of beauty. "As there is a great diversity of proportions possible, and different kinds of uniformity, so there is room enough for that diversity of fancies observable in architecture, gardening, and such like arts in different nations: they all have uniformity, though the parts in one may differ from those in another." [24] Thus "men may have different fancies of beauty, and yet uniformity be the universal foundation of our approbation of any form whatsoever as beautiful." [25] A Frenchman may like his garden regular; an Englishman prefers relative disorder. One prefers classical architecture, another baroque. But it is not about the presence or absence of beauty that they differ; for all these styles contain uniformity amidst the variety of their respective parts (more or less). "Beauty," in fact, is a term of such broad application for Hutcheson that there is scarcely a form imaginable to which it could not be applied in some degree – a point which his contemporary critics were quick to make.[26] What object, after all, cannot be said to possess, one way or another, *uniformity amidst variety*?

In Hutcheson's scheme, then, a wide divergence of tastes is consistent with the universality of the aesthetic sense. But this diversity in no way implies aesthetic anarchy. For even if few objects are completely devoid of beauty, there is nonetheless a considerable difference in degree: "there may be real beauty where there is not the greatest...." [27] Hutcheson introduces both into his ethical and aesthetic theory a kind of calculus whereby such degrees can be computed. With regard to degrees of beauty (which of course are a function of unity and variety) Hutcheson provides two basic rules: (1) that "variety increases the beauty in equal

[23] Immanuel Kant, *Critique of Aesthetic Judgement*, trans. J. C. Meredith (Oxford: Oxford University Press, 1911), p. 82.
[24] Hutcheson, *Inquiry Concerning Beauty, Order, Harmony, Design*, Section III, Article VIII.
[25] *Ibid.*, Section VI, Article VII.
[26] The point was made, for example, by Charles Louis De Villette. See A. O. Aldridge, "A French Critic of Hutcheson's Aesthetics," *Modern Philology*, XLV (1948), p. 176.
[27] Hutcheson, *Inquiry Concerning Beauty, Order, Harmony, Design*, Section VI, Article VII.

uniformity"; and (2) that "The greater uniformity increases the beauty amidst equal variety. . . ." So, to take one of Hutcheson's examples, "The beauty of an equilateral triangle is less than that of the square . . ." by rule (1): they both possess the same degree of unity whereas the square possesses greater variety (presumably because it has an extra side).[28]

There is, then, one class of disagreements in taste which does not concern the presence or absence of beauty, but merely the degree to which beauty is present. A square is more beautiful than an equilateral triangle; and although it is "correct" to assert that an equilateral triangle is beautiful, it is not "correct" to assert that an equilateral triangle is more beautiful than a square. In addition, Hutcheson seems to assume that there is a class of objects devoid of beauty which are mistakenly thought beautiful, as well as a class of beautiful objects mistakenly thought deformed. And with regard to all three of these classes, the question naturally arises: If there is a *common* sense of beauty, how can these deviations from "correct" taste be explained? Hutcheson's answer is that such aberrations are born of individual experiences of unusual and unexpected kinds, pleasant or unpleasant as the case may be, which are forever *associated* with other ideas, their chance companions: "associations of ideas make objects pleasant and delightful which are not naturally apt to give any such pleasures; and the same way, the casual conjunctions of ideas may give a disgust where there is nothing disagreeable in the form itself." [29]

Hutcheson has appropriated for aesthetics a notion that was not new to English philosophy (or, for that matter, to the common experience of mankind). The *association of ideas* had been described in the seventeenth century by Hobbes and Locke; Hutcheson, no doubt, was familiar with both accounts. Hobbes had written of association in *Human Nature* (1650) as well as in *Leviathan*; and Locke added to the fourth edition of the *Essay Concerning Human Understanding* (1700) a chapter called "Of the Association of Ideas" which became the early eighteenth century's "text" on the subject. Locke wrote:

Some of our ideas have a *natural* correspondence and connexion one with another. . . . Besides this, there is another connexion of ideas wholly owing to *chance* or *custom*. Ideas that in themselves are not all of kin, come to be so united in men's minds, that it is very hard to separate them; they always keep in company

---

[28] *Ibid.*, Section II, Article III.
[29] *Ibid.*, Section VI, Article III.

and the one no sooner at any time comes into the understanding, but its associate appears with it.... [30]

The "chance connexion of ideas" is the note to which Hutcheson tunes; and Locke provides him with an instructive example:

A grown person surfeiting with honey no sooner hears the name of it, but his fancy immediately carries sickness and qualms to his stomach, and he cannot bear the very ideas of it; ... but he knows from whence to date his weakness, and can tell how he got his indisposition. Had this happened to him by an over-dose of honey when he was a child, all the same effects would have followed; but the cause would have been mistaken, and the antipathy counted natural.[31]

It is but a step, for Hutcheson, from the taste of honey to the taste for beauty: "The *association of ideas* ... is one great cause of the apparent diversity of fancies in the sense of beauty, as well as in the external senses, and often makes men have an aversion to objects of beauty, and a liking to others void of it, but under different conceptions than those of beauty or deformity." [32] Thus the association of ideas is, for Hutcheson, the major culprit in the corruption of aesthetic sensibility by experience. He would have applauded Coleridge's assertion of almost a century later that beauty "is frequently produced by the mere removal of associations" – *produced*, here, in the sense of *revealed*.[33] What is acquired pollutes rather than purifies; what is innate had better be left alone. Hutcheson recognized, of course, that custom can quicken perception and education broaden it; but the effect is more often than not an evil one: "however custom may increase our power of receiving or comparing complex ideas, yet is seems rather to weaken than strengthen the ideas of beauty, or the impressions of pleasure from regular objects...." [34] There is a mistrust on the part of Hutcheson of the civilizing process; it corrodes the pure aesthetic metal within us. This mistrust was dispelled for a time in England by the associationist psychology which, ironically, Hutcheson helped to promulgate; and later aestheticians, chary of such imponderables as "innate senses," put their trust in an acquired "sense" when in a sense at all.

[30] John Locke, *Essay Concerning Human Understanding*, ed. A. C. Fraser (New York: Dover Publications, 1959), vol. I, p. 529.

[31] *Ibid.*, vol. I, p. 531.

[32] Hutcheson, *Inquiry Concerning Beauty, Order, Harmony, Design*, Section VI, Article XI.

[33] S. T. Coleridge, "On the Principles of Genial Criticism Concerning the Fine Arts," *Biographia Literaria*, edited with his *Aesthetical Essays* by J. Shawcross (Oxford: Oxford University Press, 1962), vol. II, p. 232.

[34] Hutcheson, *Inquiry Concerning Beauty, Order, Harmony, Design*, Section VII, Article II.

## THE SENSE OF BEAUTY: A SECOND GLANCE

We spoke at the outset of a region of unexplored vagueness in Hutcheson's theory. The time has now arrived for at least a preliminary exploration of this territory.

The trouble in interpreting Hutcheson's aesthetic theory devolves on the crucial term "idea." Our perceptions, Locke tells us, are *ideas*; and those ideas delivered to us through the external senses are basically of two kinds: ideas of "primary" and ideas of "secondary" qualities. To complicate matters further, pleasure and pain also fall under the head of "idea" in the Lockean tradition. The word "beauty," Hutcheson maintains, "is taken for the idea raised in us." But what sort of an idea is it?

Locke defines "idea" and "quality" in the following way: "Whatsoever the mind perceives *in itself*, or is the immediate object of perception, thought, or understanding, that I call *idea*; and the power to produce any idea in our mind, I call *quality* of the subject wherein that power is." [35] There now follows the notorious distinction between ideas of primary and ideas of secondary qualities, based on the supposition (much disputed in Locke's time, as in our own) that the ideas of primary qualities *resemble* the qualities themselves:

the ideas of primary qualities of bodies are resemblances of them, and their patterns do really exist in the bodies themselves, but the ideas produced in us by these secondary qualities have no real resemblance of them at all. There is nothing like our ideas, existing in the bodies themselves. They are, in the bodies we denominate from them, only a power to produce those sensations in us: and what is sweet, blue, or warm in idea, is but the certain bulk, figure, and motion of the insensible parts, in the bodies themselves, which we call so.[36]

Did Hutcheson think of beauty as the idea of a primary or a secondary quality? In one perplexing passage, he seemingly wavers between the two and finally plumps for something somewhere in the middle. Hutcheson writes:

let it be observed that by absolute or original beauty is not understood any quality supposed to be in the object which should of itself be beautiful, without relation to any mind which perceives it. For beauty, like other names of sensible ideas,

[35] Locke, *op. cit.*, vol. I, p. 169.
[36] *Ibid.*, vol. I, p. 173. I have presented Locke's position here as it would have been understood by Berkeley and, I am sure, by Hutcheson. Whether it is the *correct* interpretation of Locke on this point is at least arguable. Cf. Reginald Jackson, "Locke's Distinction Between Primary and Secondary Qualities," *Mind*, XXXVIII (1929), reprinted in *Locke and Berkeley*, ed. C. B. Martin and D. M. Armstrong (Garden City, New York: Anchor Books, 1968).

properly denotes the *perception* of some mind; so *cold, hot, sweet, bitter,* denote the sensations in our minds, to which perhaps there is no resemblance in the objects which excite these ideas in us, however we generally imagine otherwise. The ideas of beauty and harmony, being excited upon our perception of some primary quality, and having relation to figure and time, may indeed have a nearer resemblance to objects than these sensations, which seem not so much any pictures of objects as modifications of the perceiving mind; and yet, were there no mind with a sense of beauty to contemplate objects, I see not how they could be called beautiful.[37]

There is something both absurd and at the same time suggestive about this passage: absurd because if it is odd to talk about ideas being little pictures of objects, it is compounding a felony to talk about good pictures and bad pictures, or (worse still) pictures and almost-pictures; suggestive because there is a valid point being groped for here which the Lockean language is ill-suited to express. If the term 'beauty" denotes an idea which bears no resemblance to any external quality, then the judgment "X is beautiful" is, roughly speaking, a "subjective" judgment like "X is warm." If the term "beauty," however, denotes an idea which does indeed resemble an external quality, then the judgment "X is beautiful" is "objective." But Hutcheson, in the present passage, wavers between the two, indicating this indecision by saying that "beauty" may name an idea which has a nearer resemblance to some external quality than (say) the idea of "warmth" (which has no resemblance to any at all), and yet does not resemble any external quality as closely as (say) the idea of "squareness" resembles a square. Therefore, Hutcheson is saying (in a rather cumbersome way) that the judgment "X is beautiful" is neither purely subjective, nor purely objective, but something betwixt and between, a position that has seemed attractive to many contemporary philosophers, and which was enunciated most clearly in the eighteenth century by Kant when he claimed that the aesthetic judgment is based on feeling (so in that respect is *subjective*) but nevertheless demands agreement, that is, treats beauty as a property of objects (so in that respect is *objective*).

This suggestion, though, interesting as it is, remains, so far as I can make out, an isolated one in Hutcheson's writings; it is never taken up again, nor is it consistent with the general line of argument in the *Inquiry* and elsewhere. But if we set aside (as I think we must) the possibility that the idea of beauty is the idea of a primary quality, or that it has some shadowy existence between the ideas of primary and secondary

[37] Hutcheson, *Inquiry Concerning Beauty, Order, Harmony, Design*, Section I, Article XVI.

qualities, we are not, by any means, home free. A considerable range of possibilities still remains. C. D. Broad has made some valuable distinctions in the realm of moral-sense ethics which, I think, will be useful in illustrating this.

Broad divides moral-sense theories (and theories of perception in general) into two main classes: the Naively Realistic Account and the Dispositional Account. Consider, for example, the statement "That thing is yellow." In interpreting such a statement, Naively Realistic and Dispositional Accounts have this in common: a certain property is ascribed to the thing perceived and a certain property to the perceiver. Broad calls these properties, respectively, the "objective" and the "subjective correlate." [38] When a certain rapport is struck between a person and a thing, "the subjective correlate in the person and the objective correlate in the thing together cause the thing to present a yellow appearance to the person." But the "objective" and "subjective correlate" are interpreted differently on the Naively Realistic and Dispositional Accounts. For the naive realist,

the objective correlate just is that quality of sensible yellowness which, according to that theory, is spread out over the surface of the thing ready to be presented whenever the appropriate revelatory conditions are fulfilled. The subjective correlate just is the power of prehending the yellowness of yellow things when such conditions are fulfilled.

For the Dispositional Account, on the other hand,

the objective correlate is generally held to be a certain kind of minute structure and internal agitation in a thing which is not itself literally and non-dispositionally coloured. Again, the subjective correlate is not now the power of prehending the objective correlate. We have no such power. It is the capacity to have sensations of a certain kind, called "sensations of yellowness"; and these are not prehensions of a quality of yellowness inherent in the thing perceived. There is no such quality.[39]

Accepting, as he does, the Lockean paradigm of perception, Hutcheson must be considered in Broad's terms to be giving essentially a Dispositional Account of aesthetic perception; for even if the idea of beauty is the idea of a primary quality, the statement "X is beautiful" cannot be interpreted in a naively realistic way. Take the statement "X is p," where p is either a Lockean primary or secondary quality (or, for that

---

[38] C. D. Broad, "Some Reflections on Moral-Sense Theories in Ethics," reprinted in *Readings in Ethical Theory*, ed. Wilfred Sellars and John Hospers (New York: Appleton Century Crofts, 1952), p. 368.
[39] *Ibid.*, p. 369.

matter, anything betwixt and between). For the naive realist, the "subjective correlate" would be the power of prehending $p$. But for the Lockean we do not possess the power of prehending $p$; we possess only the capacity of having "ideas" of $p$. To be sure, if $p$ is a primary quality, the idea we have, although not identical with $p$, will "resemble" $p$. Thus something "like" $p$ will be "inherent in the thing perceived"; and we might want to say that in some sense or other therefore X is "non-dispositionally" $p$. Of course, if $p$ is not a primary quality, the Lockean interpretation of "X is $p$" will coincide exactly with the Dispositional Account.

Broad further divides the Dispositional Account into two subclasses: "The dispositional form of the Moral Sense Theory would take moral feeling to be either (*a*) a special kind of emotion or (*b*) a sensation analogous to those of taste or smell and not to those of sight." [40] Assuming that for Hutcheson the idea of beauty is not the idea of a primary quality and, therefore, that he is giving a completely Dispositional Account of aesthetic perception, we must now inquire which, if either, of these versions Hutcheson maintains. The answer is not at all clear.

Hutcheson frequently associates the idea of beauty with pleasure. In the Preface to the *Inquiry*, in fact, he states his purpose to be an examination of "the various pleasures which human nature is capable of receiving." The term "emotion" is not a part of the vocabulary of the *Inquiry*; and if we translate Broad's distinction into Hutcheson's language, I think it is the rather ubiquitous term "pleasure" that we must accept as its approximate synonym in this particular context. Our question then becomes: Does Hutcheson maintain the idea of beauty to be (*a*) a "pleasure" or (*b*) the idea of a secondary quality like "sweet" or "hot"? I believe there are (at least) three possible interpretations of Hutcheson on this point.

Hutcheson may be maintaining that the idea of beauty gives rise to a pleasure. He writes, for example, "the ideas of beauty and harmony, like other sensible ideas, are *necessarily* pleasant to us, as well as immediately so." [41] His position then could be stated in the following way:

[40] *Ibid.*, p. 370. Sensations of sight are ruled out by Broad simply to avoid any suggestion here of naive realism. "I suppose," he says, "that hardly anyone would put a naively realistic interpretation on such perceptual judgments as 'That is bitter' even if he were inclined to put such an interpretation on judgments like 'That is Yellow.'" But since Hutcheson, following the traditional interpretation of Locke, would not put a naively realistic interpretation on either kind of judgment, we can ignore Broad's proscription.

[41] Hutcheson, *Inquiry Concerning Beauty, Order, Harmony, Design*, Section I, Article XIII.

objects give rise (directly or indirectly) to an idea which in turn gives
rise to a pleasure. "Beauty," however, is the name for the *idea*, not the
*pleasure*. (The pleasure, of course, is also an "idea" in the Lockean
terminology – but not the idea of beauty.) In this case Hutcheson would
be giving a Dispositional Account of type (*b*). Beauty would be the idea
of a secondary quality.

But Hutcheson often expresses himself in ways which suggest that
pleasure itself (or *a* pleasure) is the sum and substance of the idea of
beauty. Thus he writes in one instance, "some objects are *immediately*
the occasions of this pleasure of beauty, and ... we have senses fitted
for perceiving it. ..." [42] Surely the implication of such a passage is that
the idea of beauty is a species of pleasure. For, presumably, the object
of the sense of beauty is beauty; and if it is pleasure that the sense of
beauty is "fitted" to perceive – is its object – then pleasure and beauty
are one and the same. In Hutcheson's later works – notably the *Essay
on the Nature and Conduct of the Passions and Affections* (1728) and
the *Short Introduction to Moral Philosophy* (1747) – this seems to be
the position which is intended more often than not, and we find Hutcheson referring to the sense of beauty in the *Introduction* as that "by
which we ... receive pleasures." [43] On this interpretation Hutcheson
could be said to maintain a Dispositional Account of type (*a*) and would
thus be inclining towards Hume's position, as stated in the *Treatise of
Human Nature*, that "pleasure and pain ... are not only necessary attendants of beauty and deformity, but constitute their very essence." [44]

It is significant, too, that in the fourth edition of the *Inquiry* (1738)
Hutcheson makes a sharp distinction at one point between pleasure and
the ideas of primary and secondary qualities, clearly associating the idea
of beauty with the former. He was obviously aware, here, of a possible
ambiguity in his position which perhaps he was not aware of earlier.
"The bare idea of form," he writes, "is something separable from
pleasure, as may appear from the different *tastes* of men about the
beauty of forms, where we don't imagine that they differ in any ideas,
either of the primary or secondary qualities." [45] That is to say, we differ

[42] *Ibid.*, Section I, Article XIV.

[43] Francis Hutcheson, *A Short Introduction to Moral Philosophy* (London,
1747), p. 13. This is an anonymous translation, usually attributed to Hutcheson
himself, of his *Philosophiae Moralis Institutio Compendiaria* (1742).

[44] David Hume, *A Treatise of Human Nature*, ed. L. A. Selby-Bigge (Oxford:
Oxford University Press, 1955), p. 299.

[45] Hutcheson, *Inquiry Concerning Beauty, Order, Harmony, Design*, Section I,
Article XII. See W. R. Scott, *Francis Hutcheson: His Life, Teaching and Position
in the History of Philosophy* (Cambridge: Cambridge University Press, 1900), pp.
216-217.

with regard to the beauty of an object not because we differ in our perceptions of any primary or secondary qualities but because we differ in our perceptions of pleasure, the conclusion being, one would think, that if beauty is an idea, it must be a pleasure. Yet scarcely a page further on, Hutcheson frustrates our expectations by repeating unaltered the statement quoted above to the effect that the idea of beauty *gives rise to a pleasure*, implying, of course, that it is *not* identical with pleasure. Thus the same perplexing vagueness returns.

But there is yet another interpretation possible – one which historical considerations tend to support, and which transforms this inconsistency of Hutcheson's into a *seeming* one only. Our problem is, essentially, to wring out of Hutcheson a position based upon the distinction between pleasure and the ideas of secondary qualities such as *sweet* or *hot* with which they might be associated. It may well be that the attempt is misguided simply because at this time Hutcheson recognized no such distinction. Now there is in Locke a very clear distinction between ideas of pleasure or pain and other ideas which give rise to them. Locke writes in the *Essay Concerning Human Understanding*: "Delight or uneasiness, one or the other of them, join themselves to almost all our ideas both of sensation and reflection: and there is scarce any affection of our senses from without, or any retired thought of our mind within, which is not able to produce in us pleasure or pain." [46] But Berkeley, some twenty years later, in the *Three Dialogues Between Hylas and Philonous* (1713), has completely obliterated the distinction between such secondary qualities as *heat* and what Locke thought of as their *consequent* pleasures or pains. So Philonous, Berkeley's advocate, argues that "the fire affects you only with one simple, uncompounded idea ... this same simple idea is both the intense heat immediately perceived, and the pain; and, consequently ... the intense heat immediately perceived, is nothing distinct from a particular sort of pain." [47]

The relevance to Hutcheson's aesthetic theory is clear: we have difficulty in discovering whether he meant by the idea of beauty a pleasure or a secondary quality because he saw no real distinction between them; both had reference to the same perceptual entity. As we would say today, the idea of beauty is a pleasure, understood under one description, a secondary quality, understood under another description: but it is one thing, not two. The beautiful (to paraphrase Berkeley) affects you only with one simple, or uncompounded idea; this same simple idea is both

[46] Locke, *op. cit.*, vol. I, p. 160.
[47] *The Works of George Berkeley*, ed. A. A. Luce and T. E. Jessop (London: Thomas Nelson and Sons, 1948-57), vol. II, p. 176.

the beauty immediately perceived, and the pleasure; and, consequently, beauty immediately perceived is nothing distinct from a particular sort of pleasure. At the time of the *Inquiry,* Hutcheson surely spoke the language of Locke – but perhaps the language of Berkeley as well. If that is the case, we have no right to press Broad's distinction too closely upon Hutcheson; it may not even have existed for him. Torture the text as we will, it cannot give up a secret it does not possess: it can only tell us a lie.[48]


### THEOLOGY AND THE SENSE OF BEAUTY

Kant recognized in Hutcheson one of the important philosophical forces in Enlightenment ethical theory. While still under the tutelage of the British moralists, he had written: "Hutcheson and others under the name of the moral feeling have made this the occasion for some splendid remarks." [49] And long after the moral sense had been rejected, Kant displayed in his aesthetic theory the lasting effects of the British school, with its emphasis upon the priority of feeling over reason in aesthetic judgment.

Of course, Hutcheson's emphasis upon feeling is obvious enough; yet he has not cast himself loose from rational moorings (although his hold may indeed be tenuous). Reason and the sense of beauty are united through a principle of utility and, ultimately, the Deity. For Hutcheson was, among other things, a rational theologian; and it is to the "Author of Nature" – the God of Natural Religion – that he must appeal as the source of our moral and aesthetic nature. Why, asks Hutcheson, should we be endued with a pleasure-giving sense of *uniformity amidst variety*? "There seems to be no necessary connection of our pleasing ideas of

---

[48] There is another avenue of interpretation which I have not explored at all, but which has been explored by William Frankena ("Hutcheson's Moral Sense Theory," *Journal of the History of Ideas,* XVI [1955]) and William T. Blackstone (*Francis Hutcheson and Contemporary Ethical Theory* [Athens, Georgia; The University of Georgia Press, [1965] in interpreting Hutcheson's ethical theory. We have been treating the term "beautiful" as *descriptive of, referring to,* an idea. But it may be that Hutcheson is saying, rather, that when I pronounce the judgment "beautiful" I am not describing or referring to a state of mind at all but *expressing* an attitude of mind, which is quite a different thing. There is some support for this interpretation in the text: where Hutcheson writes, for example, of "our approbation of any form whatsoever as beautiful" (*Inquiry Concerning Beauty, Order, Harmony, Design,* Section VI, Article VII); and there is probably more textual support for the parallel interpretation of the ethical theory. I am very doubtful, though, that such an interpretation of Hutcheson's aesthetic theory can really be sustained. It is well worth trying, however; but a trial of it cannot be made here.

[49] Schilpp, *op. cit.,* p. 32.

beauty with the uniformity or regularity of the objects, from the nature of things, antecedent to some constitution of the Author of our nature, which has made such forms pleasant to us." [50] The answer can lie only in the assumption of a *wise* and *good* Creator.

In the realm of theoretical beauty, we see that the aesthetic sense serves a clear-cut utilitarian purpose. The quest for natural causes is motivated by, among other things, a desire for practical results that such knowledge can bring – as Bacon tells us, for "the benefit and use of men ... for the glory of the Creator and the relief of man's estate." [51] The attribution of effects to a cause represents the subsumption of *variety* under some *unity*; the result is an object of the aesthetic sense and a source, therefore, of aesthetic pleasures. Thus the good and wise Creator has given us a spur to rational endeavour in the form of an autonomous pleasure, apart from the ultimate practical benefits that such endeavour brings. Had the Creator not seen fit to establish this harmony between aesthetic pleasure and rational pursuits, "there must arise a perpetual dissatisfaction in all rational agents with themselves, since reason and interest would lead us to simple general causes while a contrary sense would make us disapprove them." [52]

But we are still left with a large class of phenomena in the realm of absolute beauty which remains unexplained. For if the beauty of rational enquiry is of practical value, it is clear that the beauty of natural objects is not. It would appear, then, that the whole realm of beauty, apart from the natural sciences (and other practical disciplines), is an overflow. The good God has provided us with a pleasure-giving sense of *unity amidst variety* for our practical benefit in rational enquiry. Whatever other pleasure it may provide is purely a matter of accident.

Clearly, it is not a happy situation for a rational theologian to have such a large "accident" lying about. Hutcheson is well aware of the problem and, in the end, is forced to turn God into a kind of indulgent Papa to resolve it. The Deity, having bestowed the sense of beauty upon us for our practical benefit, has provided natural surroundings of a kind to give us pleasure in our unpractical moments: "since the divine goodness ... has constituted our sense of beauty as it is at present, the same goodness might have determined the Great Architect to adorn this

[50] Hutcheson, *Inquiry Concerning Beauty, Order, Harmony, Design*, Section V, Article I.

[51] Francis Bacon, *The Advancement of Learning*, in *Essays, Advancement of Learning, New Atlantis, and Other Pieces*, ed. R. F. Jones (New York: Odyssey Press, 1937), p. 214.

[52] Hutcheson, *Inquiry Concerning Beauty, Order, Harmony, Design*, Section VIII, Article II.

stupendous theatre in a manner agreeable to the spectators, and that part which is exposed to the observation of men so as to be pleasant to them, especially if we suppose that he designed to discover himself to them as wise and good, as well as powerful. . . ." [53]

This theology may seem an intrusion on what one would like to have called the first "pure" work of British aesthetics (or aesthetics in general). But theology is as proper an ingredient in Hutcheson's philosophy of beauty as epistemology is in Kant's, or metaphysics in Schopenhauer's. It may not be great theology; but Hutcheson, nevertheless, made a not inconsiderable contribution to Enlightenment ethics and aesthetics, and Kant and Hume were never ashamed of acknowledging their debt to Hutcheson. Newton said that he stood on the shoulders of giants. Hutcheson was not a giant; but giants stood on his shoulders – and only a big man could have borne their weight.

[53] *Ibid.*, Section VIII, Article III.

# PREFACE TO THE TWO INQUIRIES

There is no part of philosophy of more importance than a just knowledge of human nature and its various powers and dispositions. Our late inquiries have been very much employed about our understanding, and the several methods of obtaining truth. We generally acknowledge that the importance of any truth is nothing else than its moment, or efficacy to make men happy, or to give them the greatest and most lasting pleasure; and wisdom denotes only a capacity of pursuing this end by the best means. It must surely then be of the greatest importance to have distinct conceptions of this end itself, as well as of the means necessary to obtain it, that we may find out which are the greatest and most lasting pleasures, and not employ our reason, after all our laborious improvements of it, in trifling pursuits. It is to be feared, indeed, that most of our studies, without this inquiry, will be of very little use to us; for they seem to have scarce any other tendency than to lead us into speculative knowledge itself. Nor are we distinctly told how it is that knowledge, or truth, is pleasant to us.

This consideration put the author of the following papers upon inquiring into the various pleasures which human nature is capable of receiving. We shall generally find in our modern philosophic writings nothing farther on this head than some bare division of them into *Sensible*, and *Rational*, and some trite commonplace arguments to prove the latter [more] [1] valuable than the former. Our sensible pleasures are slightly passed over and explained only by some instances of tastes, smells, sounds, or such like, which men of any tolerable reflection generally look upon as very trifling satisfactions. Our rational pleasures have had much the same kind of treatment. We are seldom taught any other notion of rational pleasure than that which we have upon reflecting

[1] "to be more" – 1st ed.

on our possession, or claim to those objects which may be occasions of pleasure. Such objects we call advantageous; but advantage, or interest, cannot be distinctly conceived till we know what those pleasures are which advantageous objects are apt to excite, and what senses or powers of perception we have [with respect to] [2] such objects. We may perhaps [find] [3] such an inquiry of more importance in *morals*, to prove what we call the reality of virtue, or that it is the surest happiness of the agent, than one would first imagine.

In reflecting upon our *external senses*, we plainly see that our perceptions of pleasure or pain do not depend directly upon our will. Objects do not please us according as we incline they should. The presence of some objects necessarily pleases us, and the presence of others as necessarily displeases us. Nor can we by our will any otherwise procure pleasure or avoid pain than by procuring the former kind of objects and avoiding the latter. By the very frame of our nature the one is made the occasion of delight and the other of dissatisfaction.

The same observation will hold in all our other pleasures and pains. For there are many other sorts of objects which please or displease us as necessarily, as material objects do when they operate on our organs of sense. [There are few objects which are not thus] [4] constituted the necessary occasion of some pleasure or pain. Thus we [find] [5] ourselves pleased with a regular form, a piece of architecture or painting, a composition of notes, a theorem, an action, an affection, a character. And we are conscious that this pleasure necessarily arises from the contemplation of the idea which is then present to our minds, with all its circumstances, although some of these ideas have nothing of what we [commonly] [6] call sensible perception in them; and in those which have, the pleasure arises from some *uniformity, order, arrangement, imitation,* and not from the simple ideas of *colour* or *sound* or *mode of extension* separately considered.

These determinations to be pleased with [certain complex forms] [7] the author chooses to call *senses*, distinguishing them from the powers which commonly go by that name by calling our power of perceiving the *beauty* of regularity, order, harmony, an *internal sense*, and that determi-

----

[2] "about" – 1st ed.
[3] "see reason to imagine" – 1st ed.
[4] "There is scarcely any object which our minds are employed about which is not thus" – 1st, 2nd, and 3rd eds.
[5] "shall find" – 1st ed.
[6] Word in brackets added in 3rd ed.
[7] "any forms or ideas which occur to our observation" – 1st, 2nd, and 3rd eds.

nation to [approve] [8] affections, actions, or characters of rational agents, which we call *virtuous,* he marks by the name of a *moral sense.*

His principal design is to show that human nature was not left quite indifferent in the affair of virtue, to form to itself observations concerning the advantage or disadvantage of actions, and accordingly to regulate its conduct. The weakness of our reason, and the avocations arising from the infirmities and necessities of our nature, are so great that very few [men could ever] [9] have formed those long deductions of reason which show some actions to be in the whole advantageous to the agent, and their contraries pernicious. The Author of nature has much better furnished us for a virtuous conduct than [some] [10] moralists seem to imagine, by almost as quick and powerful instructions as we have for the preservation of our bodies. [He has given us strong affections to be the springs of each virtuous action, and made virtue a lovely form, that we might easily distinguish it from its contrary, and be made happy by the pursuit of it.] [11]

This moral sense of beauty in actions and affections may appear strange at first view. Some of our moralists themselves are offended at it in my Lord Shaftesbury, so much are they accustomed to deduce every approbation or aversion from rational views of [private] [12] interest (except it be merely in the simple ideas of the external senses) and have such a horror at *innate ideas,* which they imagine this borders upon. But this moral sense has no relation to innate ideas, as will appear in the second Treatise. Our gentlemen of good taste can tell us of a great many senses, tastes, and relishes for beauty, harmony, imitation in painting and poetry; and may not we find too in mankind a relish for a beauty in characters, in manners? [It will perhaps be found that the greater part of the ingenious arts are calculated to please some natural powers pretty different either from what we commonly call *reason,* or the external senses.] [13]

In the first Treatise the author perhaps in some instances has gone

---

[8] "be pleased with the contemplation of those" – 1st and 2nd eds.

[9] "of mankind could" – 1st ed.

[10] "our" – 1st, 2nd, and 3rd eds.

[11] "He has made virtue a lovely form, to excite our pursuit of it, and has given us strong affections to be the springs of each virtuous action" – 1st and 2nd eds.

[12] Word in brackets added in 4th ed.

[13] "I doubt we have made philosophy, as well as religion, by our foolish management of it, so austere and ungainly a form that a gentleman cannot easily bring himself to like it; and those who are strangers to it can scarcely bear to hear our description of it. So much it is changed from what was once the delight of the finest gentlemen among the ancients, and their recreation after the hurry of public affairs!" – 1st, 2nd, and 3rd eds.

too far in supposing a greater agreement of mankind in their sense of beauty than experience will [confirm]; [14] but all he is sollicitous about is to show that there is some sense of beauty natural to men; [that we find] [15] as great an agreement of men in their relishes of forms as in their external senses, which all agree to be natural; and that pleasure or pain, delight or aversion, are naturally joined to their perceptions. If the reader be convinced of [this],[16] it will be no difficult matter to apprehend another superior sense, natural also to men, determining them to be pleased with actions, characters, affections. This is the moral sense which makes the subject of the second Treatise.

The proper occasions of perception by the external senses occur to us as soon as we come into the world, [whence] [17] perhaps we easily look upon these senses to be natural; but the objects of the superior senses of beauty and virtue generally do not. It is probably some little time before children [reflect] [18] or at least let us know that they reflect upon proportion and similitude, upon affections, characters, tempers, or come to know the external actions which are evidence of them. [Hence] [19] we imagine that their sense of beauty, and their moral sentiments of actions must be entirely owing to instruction and education; whereas it is [as] [20] easy to conceive how a character, a temper, as soon as they are observed, may be constituted by nature the necessary occasion of pleasure, or an object of approbation, as a taste or a sound, [though these objects present themselves to our observation sooner than the other].[21]

[The first impression of these papers was so well received that the author hopes it will be no offence to any who are concerned in the memory of the late Lord Viscount Molesworth, if he lets his readers know that he was the noble person mentioned in the Preface to the first edition, and that their being published was owing to his approbation of them. It was from him he had that shrewd objection which the reader may find in the first Treatise,* besides many other remarks in the frequent conversations with which he honoured the author, by which

[14] "perhaps confirm" – 1st ed.
[15] "and find to the full" – 1st ed.
[16] "such determinations of the mind to be pleased with forms, proportions, resemblances, theorems" – 1st, 2nd, and 3rd eds.
[17] "and thence" – 1st ed.
[18] "do reflect" – 1st ed.
[19] "And hence" – 1st ed.
[20] "full as" – 1st ed.
[21] "though it be sometime before these objects present themselves to our observation" – 1st and 2nd eds.
* Section V, Article II, the last paragraph.

that Treatise was very much improved beyond what it was in the draught presented to him. The author retains the most grateful sense of his singular civilities and of the pleasure and improvement he received in his conversation, and is still fond of expressing his grateful remembrance of him; but, *Id cinerem, et manes credas curare sepultos*? [22]

To be concerned in this book can be no honour to a person so justly celebrated for the most generous sentiments of virtue and religion, delivered with the most manly eloquence; yet it would not be just toward the world should the author conceal his obligations to the Reverend Mr. Edward Syng, not only for revising these papers, when they stood in great need of an accurate review, but for suggesting several just amendments in the general scheme of morality. The author was much confirmed in his opinion of the justness of these thoughts upon finding that this gentleman had fallen into the same way of thinking before him, and will ever look upon his friendship as one of the greatest advantages and pleasures of his life.

To recommend the Lord Shaftesbury's writings to the world is a very needless attempt. They will be esteemed while any reflection remains among men. It is indeed to be wished that he had abstained from mixing with such noble performances some prejudices he had received against Christianity, a religion which gives us the truest idea of virtue, and recommends the love of God, and of mankind, as the sum of all true religion. How it would have moved the indignation of that ingenious nobleman to have found a dissolute set of men, who relish nothing in life but the lowest and most sordid pleasures, searching his writings for those insinuations against Christianity, that they might be the less restrained from their debaucheries, when at the same time their low minds are incapable of relishing those noble sentiments of virtue and honour which he has placed in so lovely a light!] [23]

---

[22] "Would you think that ashes and buried spirits care for this?"; trans. Michael Hanifin and Margit Minkin.

[23] Passage in brackets added in 2nd ed. There follows here another paragraph, also added in the 2nd ed., but dropped from the 4th, which reads: "In the first edition of this book there were some mistakes in one or two of the instances borrowed from other sciences, to a perfect knowledge of which the author does not pretend; nor would he now undertake that this edition is every way faultless. He hopes that those who are studious of the true measures of life may find his ideas of virtue and happiness tolerably just, and that the profound connoisseurs will pardon a few faults, in the illustrations borrowed from their arts, upon which his arguments do not depend." Preceding the bracketed passage, in the 1st ed. only, is the following:

"Were not the author diffident of his own performance, as too inconsiderable to have any great names mentioned in it, he would have publicly acknowledged his obligations to a certain Lord (whose name would have had no small authority

Whatever faults the ingenious may find with [this performance, the author] [24] hopes nobody will find anything in it contrary to religion, or good manners; and he shall be well pleased if he gives the learned world an occasion of examining more thoroughly these subjects, which are, he presumes, of very considerable importance. The chief ground of his assurance that his opinions in the main are just, is this, that as he took the first hints of them from some of the greatest writers of antiquity, so the more he has conversed with them, he finds his illustrations the more conformable to their sentiments.

[(In the later editions),[25] what alterations are made are partly owing to the objections of some gentlemen who wrote very keenly against several principles in this book. The author was convinced of some in- accurate expressions, which are now altered; and some arguments, he hopes, are now made clearer. But he has not yet seen cause to renounce any of the principles maintained in it. Nor is there anything of conse- quence added, except in Section II of Treatise 2nd; and the same reason- ing is found in Section I of the *Essay on the Passions*.] [26]

---

with the learned world) for admitting him into his acquaintance, and giving him some remarks in conversation, which have very much improved these papers be- yond what they were at first. The author might have found good materials for a modern dedication from the active parts of his life, as well as from his learning and reflection; but he knows him to be one of that sort,
 *Cui male si palpere, recalcitrat undique tutus.*
And therefore, when they come to his hands again, he only repeats to him the old dedication with which he first presented them:
 *Si quid ego adjuvero, curamve levasso,*
 *Si quae te coquat, aut verset in pectore fixa,*
 *Jam pretium tulerium.*
"The same consideration hinders the author from mentioning a clergyman to whom he was much obliged for revising these papers, and for some valuable re- marks. That gentleman's character is further known from every quality becoming his office, than the author can well presume his papers ever shall be; and therefore he thinks he can do him no honour by mentioning him."
 The sources of the Latin quotations (supplied by Hutcheson) are (respectively) Horace, *Satires*, Book II, Satire i, verse 20, and Cicero, *De Senectute, In Initio.* The line from Horace, translated by H. R. Fairclough, reads: "Stroke the steed clumsily and back he kicks, at every point on his guard." The passage from Cicero, which begins *De Senectute*, is itself a quotation from Ennius, *Annales*, Book I. It reads (in the translation of W. A. Falconer):
 ... should some aid of mine dispel
 The cares that now within thy bosom dwell
 And wring thy heart and torture thee with pain,
 What then would be the measure of my gain?
Hutcheson's Latin text differs somewhat from the one of which this is a translation.
 [24] "the author's performance, he" – 1st ed.
 [25] "In this third edition" – 3rd ed.
 [26] Passage in brackets added in 3rd ed.

[In this fourth edition there are additions interspersed, to prevent objections which have been published by several authors; and some mathematical expressions are left out which, upon second thoughts, appeared useless, and were disagreeable to some readers.] [27]

[27] Passage in brackets added in 4th ed.

# TREATISE I:

## AN INQUIRY CONCERNING BEAUTY, ORDER, HARMONY, DESIGN

### Section I:

*Concerning some Powers of Perception, distinct from what is generally understood by Sensation.*

To make the following observations understood, it may be necessary to premise some definitions, and observations, either universally acknowledged, or sufficiently proved by many writers both ancient and modern, concerning our perceptions called *sensations,* and the actions of the mind consequent upon them.

*Sensation*     I. Those ideas which are raised in the mind upon the presence of external objects, and their acting upon our bodies, are called *sensations.* We find that the mind in such cases is passive, and has not power directly to prevent the perception or idea, or to vary it at its reception, as long as we continue our bodies in a state fit to be acted upon by the external object.

*Different senses*     II. When two perceptions are entirely different from each other, or agree in nothing but the general idea of sensation, we call the powers of receiving those different perceptions different *senses.* Thus seeing and hearing denote the different powers of receiving the ideas of colours and sounds. And although colours have [great] [1] differences among themselves, as also have sounds, yet there is a greater agreement among the most opposite colours, than between any colour and a sound. Hence we call all colours perceptions of the same sense. All the several senses seem to have their distinct organs, except *feeling,* which is in some degree diffused over

[1] "vast" – 1st and 2nd eds.

the whole body.

*Mind, how*    III. The mind has a power of *compounding* ideas which
*active*    were received separately; of *comparing* [objects] [2] by means
of the ideas, and of observing their *relations* and *proportions*;
of *enlarging* and *diminishing* its ideas at pleasure, or in any
certain *ratio* or degree; and of considering *separately* each
of the simple ideas, which might perhaps have been impressed jointly in the sensation. This last operation we commonly call *abstraction*.

*Substances*    IV. The ideas of [corporeal substances] [3] are compounded
of the various simple ideas jointly impressed when they
presented themselves to our senses. We define substances
only by enumerating these sensible ideas; and such definitions may raise [a clear enough idea] [4] of the substance in
the mind of one who never immediately perceived the substance, provided he has separately received by his senses all
the simple ideas which are in the composition of the complex
one of the substance defined. [But if there be any simple
ideas which he has not received, or if he wants any of the
senses necessary for the perception of them, no definition
can raise any simple idea which has not been before perceived by the senses.] [5]

*Education.*    V. Hence it follows that when instruction, education, or
*Instruction* prejudice of any kind raise any desire or aversion toward
an object, this desire or aversion must be founded upon an
opinion of some perfection, or some deficiency in those
qualities for perception of which we have the proper senses.
Thus if beauty be desired by one who has not the sense of
sight, the desire must be raised by some apprehended regularity of figure, sweetness of voice, smoothness, or softness,
or some other quality perceivable by the other senses, without relation to the ideas of colour.

*Pleasure,*    [VI. Many of our sensitive perceptions are pleasant, and
*Pain*    many painful, immediately, and that without any knowledge
of the cause of this pleasure or pain, or how the objects

---

[2] "their objects" – 1st and 2nd eds.
[3] "substances" – 1st, 2nd, and 3rd eds.
[4] "an idea clear enough" – 1st, 2nd, and 3rd eds.
[5] "But if he has not received any of these ideas, or wants the senses necessary
for the perception of them, no definition can ever raise in him any idea of that
sense in which he is deficient" – 1st ed.

excite it, or are the occasions of it, or without seeing to what farther advantage or detriment the use of such objects might tend. Nor would the most accurate knowledge of these things vary either the pleasure or pain of the perception, however it might give a rational pleasure distinct from the sensible; or might raise a distinct joy from a prospect of farther advantage in the object, or aversion from an apprehension of evil.] [6]

*Different ideas*

VII. The [simple] [7] ideas raised in different persons by the same object are probably [some way] [8] different when they disagree in their approbation or dislike, and in the same person when his fancy at one time differs from what it was at another. This will appear from reflecting on those objects to which we have now an aversion, though they were formerly agreeable. And we shall generally find that there is some accidental conjunction of a disagreeable idea which always recurs with the object, as in those wines [to which men acquire an aversion] [9] after they have taken them in an emetic preparation, [we] [10] are conscious that the idea is altered from what it was when that wine was agreeable, by the conjunction of the ideas of loathing and sickness of the stomach. The like change of idea may be insensibly made by the change of our bodies as we advance in years, [or when we are accustomed to any object,] [11] which may occasion an indifference toward meats we were fond of in our childhood, [and may make some objects cease to raise the disagreeable ideas which they excited upon our first use of them. Many of our simple perceptions are disagreeable only through the too great intenseness of the quality: thus moderate light is agreeable, very strong light may be painful; moderate bitter may be pleasant, a higher degree may be offensive. A change in our organs will necessarily occasion a change in the intenseness of the perception at least, nay sometimes will occasion a quite contrary perception: thus a warm hand shall feel that water cold which a cold hand shall feel warm.] [12]

[6] Passage in brackets occupied the position of article V in 1st ed.
[7] Word in brackets added in 2nd ed.
[8] Words in brackets added in 2nd ed.
[9] "which men acquire an aversion to" – 1st ed.
[10] "In this case we" – 1st and 2nd eds.
[11] Passage in brackets added in 2nd ed.
[12] Passage in brackets added in 2nd ed.

We shall not find it perhaps so easy to account for the diversity of fancy [about more complex ideas of objects, (including many) [13] in which we regard many ideas of different senses at once, as (some) [14] perceptions of those called *primary qualities,* and some *secondary,* as explained by Mr. Locke: for instance, in the different fancies about architecture, gardening, dress. Of the two former, we shall offer something in Sect. VI. As to dress, we may generally account for the diversity of fancies from a like conjunction of ideas. Thus] [15] if either from anything in nature, or from the opinion of our country or acquaintance, the fancying of glaring colours be looked upon as an evidence of levity, or of any other evil quality of mind, or if any colour or fashion be commonly used by rustics, or by men of any disagreeable profession, employment, or temper, these additional ideas may recur constantly with that of the colour or fashion, and cause a constant dislike to them in those who join the additional ideas, although the colour or form be no way disagreeable of themselves, and actually do please others who join no such ideas to them. But there [appears no] [16] ground to believe such a diversity in human minds, as that the same simple idea or perception should give pleasure to one and pain to another, or to the same person at different times, not to say that it seems a contradiction that the same simple idea should do so.

*Complex ideas*    VIII. The only pleasure of sense which [many] [17] philosophers seem to consider is that which accompanies the simple ideas of sensation. But there are [far] [18] greater pleasures in those complex ideas of objects, which obtain the names of *beautiful, regular, harmonious.* Thus every one acknowledges he is more delighted with a fine face, a just picture, than with the view of any one colour, were it as strong and lively as possible; and more pleased with a prospect of the sun arising among settled clouds, and colouring their edges with a starry hemisphere, a fine landscape, a regular

---

[13] Words in parentheses added in 4th ed.
[14] "in some" – 2nd and 3rd eds.
[15] "in our dress, and some other affairs; and yet this may arise from a like accidental conjunction of ideas: as for instance" – 1st ed.
[16] "does not seem to be any" – 1st, 2nd, and 3rd eds.
[17] "our" – 1st and 2nd eds.
[18] "vastly" – 1st and 2nd eds.

building, than with a clear blue sky, a smooth sea, or a large open plain, not diversified by woods, hills, waters, buildings. And yet even these latter appearances are not quite simple. So in music, the pleasure of fine composition is incomparably greater than that of any one note, how sweet, full, or swelling soever.

*Beauty*

*Harmony*

IX. Let it be observed that in the following papers the word *beauty* is taken for *the idea raised in us,* and a *sense* of beauty for *our power of receiving this idea. Harmony* also denotes *our pleasant ideas arising from composition of sounds,* and a *good ear* (as it is generally taken) a *power of perceiving this pleasure.* In the following sections, an attempt is made to discover what is the immediate occasion of these pleasant ideas, or what real quality in the objects ordinarily excites them.

*Internal sense*

X. It is of no consequence whether we call these ideas of beauty and harmony perceptions of the external senses of seeing and hearing, or not. I should rather choose to call our power of perceiving these ideas an *internal sense,* were it only for the convenience of distinguishing them from other sensations of seeing and hearing which men may have without perception of beauty and harmony. It is plain from experience that many men have in the common meaning the senses of seeing and hearing perfect enough. They perceive all the *simple ideas* separately, and have their pleasures; they distinguish them from each other, such as one colour from another, either quite different, or the stronger or fainter of the same colour, [when they are placed beside each other, although they may often confound their names when they occur apart from each other, as some do the names of green and blue.] [19] They can tell in separate notes, the higher, lower, sharper or flatter, when separately sounded; in figures they discern the length, breadth, wideness of each line, surface, angle; and may be as capable of hearing and seeing at great distances as any men whatsoever. And yet perhaps they shall find no pleasure in musical compositions, in painting, architecture, natural landscape, or but a very weak one in comparison of what others enjoy from the same objects. This greater capacity of receiving such pleasant

[19] Passage in brackets added in 2nd ed.

ideas we commonly call a *fine genius* or *taste*. In music we seem universally to acknowledge something like a distinct sense from the external one of hearing, and call it a *good ear*; and the like distinction we should probably acknowledge in other [objects,] [20] had we also got distinct names to denote these *powers* of perception by.

*Different from external*

XI. [We generally imagine the brute animals endowed with the same sort of powers of perception as our external senses, and having sometimes greater acuteness in them; but we conceive few or none of them with any of these sublimer powers of perception here called *internal senses,* or at least if some of them have them, it is in a degree much inferior to ours.] [21]

There will appear another reason perhaps hereafter for calling this power of perceiving the ideas of beauty an *internal sense,* from this, that in some other affairs where our external senses are not much concerned, we discern a sort of beauty, very like, in many respects, to that observed in sensible objects, and accompanied with like pleasure. Such is that beauty perceived in theorems, or universal truths, in general causes, and in some extensive principles of action.

XII. [Let one consider, first, that 'tis probable a being may have the full power of external sensation, which we enjoy, so as to perceive each colour, line, surface, as we do; yet, without the power of *comparing,* or of discerning the similitudes of proportions. Again, it might discern these also, and yet have no pleasure or delight accompanying these perceptions. The bare idea of the form is something separable from pleasure, as may appear from the different *tastes* of men about the beauty of forms, where we don't imagine that they differ in any ideas, either of the primary or secondary qualities. *Similitude, proportion, analogy* or *equality* of proportion are objects of the understanding, and must be actually known before we know the natural causes of our pleasure. But pleasure perhaps is not necessarily connected with perception of them, and may be felt where the proportion is not known or attended to, and may not be felt where the proportion is observed.][22] Since then there are

[20] "affairs" – 1st ed.
[21] Passage in brackets added in 4th ed.
[22] "Let everyone here consider how different we must suppose the perception

such different powers of perception, where what are commonly called *external* senses are the same, since the most accurate knowledge of what the external senses discover [may often] [23] not give the pleasure of beauty or harmony which yet one of a good taste will enjoy at once without much knowledge, we may justly use another name for these higher and more delightful perceptions of beauty and harmony, and call the *power* of receiving such impressions an *internal sense*. The difference of the perceptions seems sufficient to vindicate the use of a different name, [especially when we are told in what meaning the word is applied.] [24]

*Its pleasures necessary and immediate*  This superior power of perception is justly called a *sense* because of its affinity to the other senses in this, that the pleasure does not arise from any *knowledge* of principles, proportions, causes, or of the usefulness of the object, but strikes us at first with the idea of beauty. Nor does the most accurate knowledge increase this pleasure of beauty, however it may superadd a distinct rational pleasure from prospects of advantage, or from the increase of knowledge.*

XIII. And farther, the ideas of beauty and harmony, like other sensible ideas, are *necessarily* pleasant to us, as well as immediately so. Neither can any resolution of our own, nor any prospect of advantage or disadvantage, vary the beauty or deformity of an object. For as in the external sensations, no view of interest will make an object grateful, nor [view

to be with which a poet is transported upon the prospect of any of those objects of natural beauty which ravish us even in his description, from that cold lifeless conception which we imagine [in] a dull critic, or one of the *virtuosi*, without what we call a *fine taste*. This latter class of men may have greater perfection in that knowledge which is derived from external sensation. They can tell the specific differences of trees, herbs, minerals, metals; they know the form of every leaf, stalk, root, flower, and seed of all the species, about which the poet is often very ignorant. And yet the poet shall have a much more delightful perception of the whole, and not only the poet but any man of a fine taste. Our external senses may, by measuring, teach us all the proportions of architecture to the tenth of an inch, and the situation of every muscle in the human body; and a good memory may retain these. And yet there is still something farther necessary, not only to make [a man a] complete master in architecture, painting, or statuary, but even a tolerable judge in these works, or [capable of receiving] the highest pleasure in contemplating them" – 2nd and 3rd eds. The words in brackets have alternate readings in the first edition which are as follows: "to be in"; "a"; "to receive."

[23] "often does" – 1st, 2nd, and 3rd eds.

[24] Passage in brackets added in 2nd ed.

* See above, Article VI.

of][25] detriment distinct from immediate pain in the perception, make it disagreeable to the sense. So propose the whole world as a reward, or threaten the greatest evil, to make us approve a deformed object, or disapprove a beautiful one: dissimulation may be procured by rewards or threatenings, or we may in external conduct abstain from any pursuit of the beautiful, and pursue the deformed, but our *sentiments* of the forms, and our *perceptions,* would continue invariably the same.

*This sense antecedent to, and distinct from prospects of interest* XIV. Hence it plainly appears that some objects are *immediately* the occasions of this pleasure of beauty, and that we have senses fitted for perceiving it, and that it is distinct from that *joy* which arises upon prospect of advantage. Nay, do not we often see convenience and use neglected to obtain beauty, without any other prospect of advantage in the beautiful form than the suggesting the pleasant ideas of beauty? Now this shows us that however we may pursue beautiful objects from self-love, with a view to obtain the pleasures of beauty, as in architecture, gardening, and many other affairs, yet there must be a *sense* of beauty, antecedent to prospects [even of][26] this advantage, without which sense these objects would not be thus advantageous, nor excite in us this pleasure which constitutes them advantageous. Our sense of beauty from objects, by which they are constituted good to us, is very distinct from our desire of them when they are thus constituted. Our desire of beauty may be counter-balanced by rewards of threatenings, but never our *sense* of it, even as fear of death [may make us][27] desire a bitter potion, or neglect those meats which the sense of taste would recommend as pleasant, [but cannot][28] make that potion agreeable to the *sense,* or meat disagreeable to it, which was not so antecedently to this prospect. [The same holds true of][29] the sense of beauty and harmony; that the pursuit of such objects is frequently neglected, from prospects of advantage, aversion to labour, or any other motive of [interest][30] does not prove that we

[25] Words in brackets added in 2nd ed.
[26] "of even" – 1st ed.
[27] "or love of life may make us choose and" – 1st and 2nd eds.
[28] "and yet no prospect of advantage, or fear of evil, can" – 1st, 2nd, and 3rd eds.
[29] "Just in the same manner as to" – 1st and 2nd eds.
[30] "self-love" – 1st and 2nd eds.

have no *sense* of beauty, but only that our desire of it may be counter-balanced by a stronger desire. [So gold outweighing silver is never adduced as proof that the latter is void of gravity.] [31]

XV. Had we no such sense of beauty and harmony, houses, gardens, dress, equipage might have been recommended to us as convenient, fruitful, warm, easy, but never as *beautiful*. [And in faces I see nothing which could please us but liveliness of colour and smoothness of surface.] [32] And yet nothing is more certain than that all these objects are recommended under quite different views on many occasions. ['Tis true, what chiefly pleases in the countenance are the indications of moral dispositions; and yet, were we by the longest acquaintance fully convinced of the best moral dispositions in any person, with that countenance we now think deformed, this would never hinder our immediate dislike of the form, or our liking other forms more.] [33] [And custom, education, or example could never] [34] give us perceptions distinct from those of the senses which we had the use of before, or recommend objects under another conception than grateful to * them. But of the influence of custom, education, example, upon the sense of beauty, we shall treat below.**

*Beauty original or comparative*

XVI. Beauty [in corporeal forms] [35] is either *original* or *comparative*; or, if any like the terms better, *absolute* or *relative*. Only let it be [observed] [36] that by absolute or original beauty is not understood any quality supposed to be in the object [which] [37] should of itself be beautiful, without relation to any mind which perceives it. For beauty, like other names of sensible ideas, properly denotes the *perception* of some mind; so *cold*, [*hot*,] [38] *sweet*, *bitter*, denote the sensations in our minds, to which perhaps there is no resemblance in the objects which excite these ideas in us,

[31] Passage in brackets deleted in 3rd and 4th eds.
[32] Passage in brackets deleted in 4th ed.
[33] Passage in brackets added in 4th ed.
[34] "And no custom, education, or example could ever" – 1st and 2nd eds.
* See Article VI.
** Section VII.
[35] Words in brackets added in 4th ed.
[36] "noted" – 1st ed.
[37] "that" – 1st ed.
[38] "*heat*" – 1st ed.

however we generally imagine [otherwise.] [39] The ideas of beauty and harmony, being excited upon our perception of some primary quality, and having relation to figure and time, may indeed have a nearer resemblance to objects than these sensations, which seem not so much any pictures of objects as modifications of the perceiving mind; and yet, were there no mind with a sense of beauty to contemplate objects, I see not how they could be called beautiful. We therefore by * [40] absolute beauty understand only that beauty which we perceive in objects without comparison to anything external, of which the object is supposed an imitation or picture, such as that beauty perceived from the works of nature, artificial forms, [figures].[41] Comparative or relative beauty is that which we perceive in objects commonly considered as *imitations* or *resemblances* of something else. These two kinds of beauty employ the three following sections.

## Section II:

### *Of Original or Absolute Beauty*

*Sense*
*of men*

I. Since it is certain that we have *ideas* of beauty and harmony, let us examine what *quality* in objects excites these ideas, or is the occasion of them. And let it be here observed that our inquiry is only about the qualities which are beautiful to *men,* or about the foundation of their sense of beauty. For as was above hinted, beauty has always relation to the sense of some mind; and when we afterwards show how generally the objects which occur to us are beautiful, we mean [that such objects are] [1] agreeable to the sense of men, for [there are many objects] [2] which seem no way beautiful to men,

---

[39] "that there is something in the object just like our perception" – 1st and 2nd eds.

* This division of beauty is taken from the different foundations of pleasure [to] our sense of it, rather than from the objects themselves; for most of the following instances of relative beauty have also absolute beauty, and many of the instances of absolute beauty have also relative beauty in some respect or other. But we may distinctly consider these two fountains of pleasure, uniformity in the object itself, and resemblance to some original.

[40] Bracketed word in footnote reads "as to" in 1st ed.

[41] "figures, theorems" – 1st, 2nd, and 3rd eds.

[1] Passage in brackets added in 2nd ed.

[2] "as there are not a few objects" – 1st and 2nd eds.

[and yet other animals] [3] seem delighted with them: they may have senses otherwise constituted than those of men, and may have the ideas of beauty excited by objects of a quite different form. We see animals fitted for every place, and what to men appears rude and shapeless, or loathsome, may be to them a paradise.

II. That we may more distinctly discover the general foundation or occasion of the ideas of beauty among men, it will be necessary to consider it first in its simpler kinds, such as occurs to us in regular figures; and we may perhaps find that the same foundation extends to all the more complex species of it.

*Uniformity with variety*   III. The figures [which] [4] excite in us the ideas of beauty seem to be those in which there is *uniformity amidst variety*. There are many conceptions of objects which are agreeable upon other accounts, such as *grandeur, novelty, sanctity,* and some others, [which shall be mentioned hereafter.*] [5] But what we call beautiful in objects, to speak in the mathematical style, seems to be in compound ratio of uniformity and variety: so that where the uniformity of bodies is equal, the beauty is as the variety; and where the variety is equal, the beauty is as the uniformity. [This may seem probable, and hold pretty generally.] [6]

*Variety*   First, the variety increases the beauty in equal uniformity. The beauty of an equilateral triangle is less than that of the square, which is less than that of a pentagon, and this again is surpassed by the hexagon. When indeed the number of sides is much increased, the proportion of them to the radius, or diameter of the figure, or of the circle to which regular polygons have an obvious relation, is so much lost to our observation, that the beauty does not always increase with the number of sides, and the want of parallelism in the sides of heptagons, and other figures of odd numbers, may also diminish their beauty. So in solids, the eicosiedron surpasses the dodecaedron, and this the octaedron, which is still more beautiful than the cube, and this again surpasses

---

[3] "so we see a variety of other animals who" – 1st and 2nd eds.
[4] "that" – 1st ed.
* See Section VI, Articles XI, XII, XIII.
[5] "that shall be touched at afterwards" – 1st ed.
[6] "This will be plain from examples" – 1st, 2nd, and 3rd eds.

the regular pyramid. The obvious ground of this is greater variety with equal uniformity.

*Uniformity*    The greater uniformity increases the beauty amidst equal variety in these instances: an equilateral triangle, or even an isosceles, surpasses the scalenum; a square surpasses the rhombus or lozenge, and this again the rhomboides, which [is] [7] still more beautiful than the trapezium, or any figure with [irregular] [8] curve sides. So the regular solids surpass all other solids of equal number of plane surfaces. And the same is observable not only in the five perfectly regular solids, but in all those which have any considerable uniformity, as cylinders, prisms, pyramids, obelisks, which please every eye more than any rude figures, where there is no unity or resemblance among the parts.

*Com-*    Instances of the compound ratio we have in comparing
*pound*    circles or spheres with ellipses or spheroids not very ec-
*ratio*    centric, and in comparing the compound solids, the exotae-dron, and eicosidodecaedron, with the perfectly regular ones of which they are compounded; and we shall find that the want of that most perfect uniformity observable in the latter is compensated by the greater variety in the [former,] [9] so that the beauty is nearly equal.

IV. These observations would probably hold true for the most part, and might be confirmed by the judgment of children in the simpler figures, where the variety is not too great for their comprehension. And however uncertain some of the particular aforesaid instances may seem, yet this is perpetually to be observed, that children are fond of all regular figures in their little diversions, although they be no more convenient or useful for them than the figures of our common pebbles. We see how early they discover a taste or sense of beauty in desiring to see buildings, regular gardens, or even representations of them in pictures of any kind.

*Beauty of*    V. [The same foundation] [10] we have for our sense of
*nature*    beauty in the works of nature. In every part of the world which we call beautiful there is a [surprising] [11] uniformity

---

[7] "yet is" – 1st ed.
[8] "irregularly" – 1st ed.
[9] "others" – 1st and 2nd eds.
[10] "It is the same foundation which" – 1st and 2nd eds.
[11] "vast" – 1st and 2nd eds.

amidst [an] [12] almost infinite variety. Many parts of the universe seem not at all designed for the use of man; nay, it is but a very small spot with which we have any acquaintance. The figures and motions of the great bodies are not obvious to our senses, but found out by reasoning and reflection, upon many long observations; and yet as far as we can by sense discover, or by reasoning enlarge our knowledge and extend our imagination, we generally find their structure, [order,] [13] and motion agreeable to our sense of beauty. Every particular object in nature does not indeed appear beautiful to us; but there is a [great] [14] profusion of beauty over most of the objects which occur either to our senses, or reasonings upon observation. For not to mention the apparent situation of the heavenly bodies in the circumference of a great sphere, which is wholly occasioned by the imperfection of our sight in discerning distances, the forms of all the great bodies in the universe are nearly spherical, the orbits of their revolutions generally elliptic, and without great eccentricity, in those which continually occur to our observation. [Now] [15] these are figures of great uniformity, and therefore pleasing to us.

Further, to pass by the less obvious uniformity in the proportion of their quantities of matter, distances, times of revolving, to each other, what can exhibit a greater instance of uniformity amidst variety than the constant tenour of revolutions in nearly equal times, in each planet around its axis, and the central fire, or sun, through all the ages of which we have any records, and in nearly the same orbit? [Thus] [16] after certain periods all the same appearances are again renewed. The alternate successions of light and shade, or day and night, constantly pursuing each other around each planet, with an agreeable and regular diversity in the times they possess the several hemispheres, in the summer, harvest, winter, and spring, and the various phases, aspects, and situations of the planets to each other, their conjunctions and oppositions, in which they suddenly darken each other

---

[12] Word in brackets added in 2nd ed.
[13] "and order" – 1st ed.
[14] "vast" – 1st and 2nd eds.
[15] "And" – 1st ed.
[16] "By which" – 1st and 2nd eds.

with their conic shades in eclipses, are repeated to us at their fixed periods with invariable constancy. These are the beauties which charm the astronomer, and make his tedious calculations pleasant.

*Molliter austerum studio fallente laborem.* *[17]

*Earth*    VI. Again, as to the the dry part of the surface of our globe, a great part of which is covered with a very pleasant inoffensive colour, how beautifully is it diversified with various degrees of light and shade, according to the different situations of the parts of its surface, in mountains, valleys, hills, and open plains, which are variously inclined toward the great luminary!

*Plants*    VII. If we descend to the minuter works of nature, what [great] [18] uniformity among all the species of plants and vegetables in the manner of their growth and propagation! [How near the] [19] resemblance among all the plants of the same species, whose numbers surpass our imagination! And this uniformity is not only observable in the form in gross (nay, in this it is not so very exact in all instances) but in the structure of their minutest parts, [even of those] [20] which no eye unassisted with glasses can discern. In the almost infinite multitude of leaves, fruit, seed, flowers of any one species we often see a very great uniformity in the structure and situation of the smallest fibres. This is the beauty which charms an ingenious botanist. Nay, what great uniformity and regularity of figure is found in each particular plant, leaf, or flower! In all trees and most of the smaller plants the stalks or trunks are either cylinders, nearly, or regular prisms, the branches similar to their several trunks, arising at nearly regular distances when no accidents retard their natural growth. In one species the branches arise in pairs on the opposite sides, the perpendicular plain of direction of the immediately superior pair intersecting the plain of direction of the inferior nearly at right angles. In another species the branches [spring] [21] singly, and alternately, all

---

* Horace, *Satires*, Book II, Satire ii, verse 12.
[17] "Where the excitement pleasantly beguiles the hard toil"; trans. H. R. Fairclough.
[18] "vast" – 1st and 2nd eds.
[19] "What exact" – 1st and 2nd eds.
[20] Passage in brackets added in 4th ed.
[21] "shall spring" – 1st ed.

around in nearly equal distances; and the branches in other species [sprout] [22] all in knots around the trunk, one for each year. And in [each] [23] species all the branches in the first shoots preserve the same angles with their trunk; and they again sprout out into smaller branches exactly after the manner of their trunks. Nor ought we to pass over that great unity of colours [which we often see] [24] in all the flowers of the same plant or tree, and often of a whole species, and their exact agreement in many shaded transitions into opposite colours, in which all the flowers of the same plant generally agree, nay often all the flowers of a species.

*Animals*    VIII. Again, as to the beauty of animals, either in their inward structure, which we come to the knowledge of by experience and long observation, or their outward form, we shall find [surprising] [25] uniformity among all the species which are known to us, in the structure of those parts upon which life depends more immediately. And how amazing is the unity of mechanism when we shall find an almost infinite diversity of motions, all their actions in walking, running, flying, swimming; all their serious efforts for self-preservation, all their freakish contortions when they are gay and sportful, in all their various limbs, performed by one simple contrivance of a contracting muscle, applied with inconceivable diversities to answer all these ends. Various engines might have obtained the same ends; but then there had been less uniformity, and the beauty of our animal systems, and of particular animals, had been much less, when this surprising unity of mechanism had been removed from them.

IX. Among animals of the same species unity is very obvious, and this resemblance is the very ground of our ranking them in such classes or species, notwithstanding the great diversities in bulk, colour, shape, which are observed even in those called of the same species. And then in each individual, [how universal is that beauty which] [26] arises from the exact resemblance of all the external double members to each other, which seems the universal intention of

[22] "shall sprout" – 1st ed.
[23] "every" – 1st and 2nd eds.
[24] Passage in brackets added in 2nd ed.
[25] "vast" – 1st and 2nd eds.
[26] "what vast beauty" – 1st and 2nd eds.

nature, when no accident prevents it! We see the want of this resemblance never fails to pass for an imperfection, and want of beauty, though no other inconvenience ensues, as when the eyes are not exactly like, or one arm or leg is a little shorter or smaller than its fellow.

[As to that most powerful beauty in countenances, airs, gestures, motion, we shall show in the second Treatise * that it arises from some imagined indication of morally good dispositions of the mind.] [27] [In motion there is also a natural beauty, when at fixed periods like gestures and steps are regularly repeated, suiting the time and air of music, which is observed in regular dancing.] [28]

*Proportion*    X. There is a farther beauty in animals, arising from a certain proportion of the various parts to each other, which still pleases the sense of spectators, though they cannot calculate it with the accuracy of a statuary. The statuary knows what proportion of each part of the face to the whole face is most agreeable, and can tell us the same of the proportion of the face to the body, or any parts of it, and between the diameters and lengths of each limb. When this proportion of the head to the body is remarkably altered, we shall have a giant or a dwarf; and hence it is that either the one or the other may be represented to us even in miniature, without relation to any external object, by observing how the body surpasses the proportion it should have to the head in giants, and falls below it in dwarfs. There is a farther beauty arising from that figure which is a natural indication of strength; but this may be passed over, because our approbation of this shape flows from [an] [29] opinion of advantage, and not from the form itself.

The beauty arising from mechanism apparently adapted to the necessities and advantages of any animal, which pleases us even though there be no advantage to ourselves ensuing from it, will be considered under the head of *Relative Beauty*, or *Design*.**

*Fowls*    XI. The peculiar beauty of fowls can scarce be omitted,

* Section VI, Article III.
[27] Passage in brackets added in 2nd ed.
[28] Passage in brackets added in 3rd ed.
[29] Word in brackets added in 2nd ed.
** See Section VI, Article XII.

which arises from the [great] [30] variety of feathers, a curious sort of machines adapted to many admirable uses, which retain a [considerable] [31] resemblance in their structure among all the species, and [frequently] [32] a perfect uniformity in those of the same species in the corresponding parts, and in the two sides of each individual, besides all the beauty of lively colours and gradual shades, not only in the external appearance of the fowl, resulting from an artful combination of shaded feathers, but often visible even in one feather separately.

*Fluids*  XII. If our reasonings about the nature of fluids be just, the vast stores of water will give us an instance of uniformity in nature above imagination, when we reflect upon the almost infinite multitude of small, polished, smooth spheres which must be supposed formed in all the parts of this globe. The same uniformity there is probably among the parts of other fluids as well as water; and the like must be observed in several other natural bodies, as salts, sulphurs, and such like, whose uniform properties do probably depend upon an uniformity in the figures of their parts.

*Harmony*  XIII. Under *original beauty* we may include *harmony,* or *beauty of sound,* if that expression can be allowed, because harmony is not usually conceived as an imitation of anything else. Harmony often raises pleasure in those who know not what is the occasion of it; and yet the foundation of this pleasure is known to be a sort of uniformity. When the several vibrations of one note regularly coincide with the vibrations of another they make an agreeable composition; and such notes are called [*concords.*] [33] Thus the vibrations of any one note coincide in time with [two vibrations] [34] of its octave; and two vibrations of any note coincide with three of its fifth, and so on in the rest of the [concords.] [35] [Now no composition can be harmonious in which the notes are not, for the most part, disposed according to these natural proportions. Besides which, a due regard must be had to

---

[30] "vast" – 1st and 2nd eds.
[31] "vast" – 1st and 2nd eds.
[32] Word in brackets added in 4th ed.
[33] "chords" – 1st ed.
[34] "every second vibration" – 1st ed.
[35] "chords" – 1st ed.

the *key*, which governs the whole, and to the *time* and *humour* in which the composition is begun, a frequent and inartificial change of any of which will produce the greatest and most unnatural discord. This will appear by observing the dissonance which would arise from tacking parts of different tunes together as one, although both were separately agreeable. A like uniformity is also observable among the *basses, tenors, trebles* of the same tune.] [36]

[There is indeed observable, in the best compositions, a mysterious effect of discords: they often give as great a pleasure as continued harmony, whether by refreshing the ear with variety, or by awakening the attention, and enlivening the relish for the succeeding harmony of concords, as shades enliven and beautify pictures, or by some other means not yet known. Certain it is, however, that they have their place, and some good effect in our best compositions.] [37] Some other powers of music may be considered hereafter.*

XIV. But in all these instances of ** [38] beauty let it be observed that the pleasure is communicated to those who never reflected on this general foundation, and that all here alleged is this, that the pleasant sensation arises only from objects in which there is *uniformity amidst variety.* We may have the sensation without knowing what is the occasion of it, as a man's taste may suggest ideas of sweets, acids, bitters, though he be ignorant of the forms of the small bodies, or their motions, which excite these perceptions in him.

---

[36] "Now good compositions, beside the frequency of these chords, must retain a general unity of key, an uniformity among the parts in bars, risings, fallings, closes. The necessity of this will appear by observing the dissonance which would arise from tacking parts of different tunes together as one, although both were separately agreeable. A greater uniformity is also observable among the basses, tenors, trebles of the same tune" – 1st ed.

[37] Passage in brackets added in 2nd ed.

* See Section IV, Article VII.

** There is nothing singular in applying the word *beauty* to sounds. The ancients observe the peculiar dignity of the sense of seeing and hearing, that in their objects we discern the Καλὸν, which we don't ascribe to the objects of the other senses.

[38] Footnote added in 4th ed.

Section III:

*Of the Beauty of Theorems*

*Theorems*  I. The beauty of *theorems,* or universal truths demonstrated, deserves a distinct consideration, [being] [1] of a nature pretty different from the former kinds of beauty; and yet there is none in which we shall see such an amazing variety with uniformity, and hence arises a very great pleasure distinct from prospects of any farther advantage.

II. For in one theorem we may find included, with the most exact agreement, an infinite multitude of particular truths, nay, often [a multitude] [2] of infinites, so that although the necessity of forming abstract ideas and universal theorems arises perhaps from the limitation of our minds which cannot admit an infinite multitude of singular ideas or judgments at once, yet this power gives us an evidence of the largeness of the human capacity above our imagination. Thus, for instance, the 47th Proposition of the first Book of Euclid's *Elements* contains an infinite multitude of truths concerning the infinite possible sizes of right-angled triangles, as you make the area greater or less; and in each of these sizes you may find an infinite multitude of dissimilar triangles, as you vary the proportion of the base to the perpendicular, all which [infinites] [3] agree in the general theorem. [In algebraic and fluxional calculations we shall (find a like) [4] variety of particular truths included in general theorems, not only in general equations applicable to all kinds of quantity, but in more particular investigations of areas and tangents, in which one manner of operation shall discover theorems applicable to (many) [5] orders of species of curves, to the infinite sizes of each species, and to the infinite points of the infinite individuals of each size.] [6]

[1] "because" – 1st ed.
[2] "an infinity" – 1st, 2nd, and 3rd eds.
[3] "infinities of infinities" – 1st, 2nd, and 3rd eds.
[4] "still find a greater" – 2nd and 3rd eds.
[5] "infinite" – 2nd and 3rd eds.
[6] "Thus also one fluxional calculation shall determine the tangents of all algebraic curves; of these curves there are infinite orders and species possible, of each species infinite sizes, or magnitudes of areas, of each size infinite individuals, of each individual curve an infinity of points from which tangents may be drawn. But all these infinities of infinites are exactly comprehended in the general theorem, which fixes the length of the subtangents, or their proportion to the abscissa" – 1st ed.

*Foun-*
*dations*
*of their*
*Beauty*

III. That we may the better discern this agreement or unity of an infinity of objects, in the general theorem, to be the foundation of the beauty or pleasure attending their discovery, let us compare our satisfaction in such discoveries with the uneasy state of [mind] [7] when we can only measure lines, or surfaces, by a scale, or are making experiments which we can reduce to no general canon, but [are] [8] only heaping up a multitude of particular incoherent observations. Now each of these trials discovers a new truth, but with no pleasure or beauty, notwithstanding the variety, till we can discover some sort of unity or reduce them to some general canon.

*Little*
*beauty*
*in axioms*

IV. Again, let us take a metaphysical axiom, such as this, *Every whole is greater than its part,* and we shall find no beauty in the contemplation. [For though this proposition contains] [9] many infinities of particular truths, yet the unity is inconsiderable, since they all agree only in a vague undetermined conception of *whole* and *part,* and in an indefinite excess of the former above the latter, which is sometimes great and sometimes small. So, should we hear that the cylinder is greater than the inscribed sphere, and this again greater than the cone of the same altitude and diameter [of] [10] the base, we shall find no pleasure in this knowledge of a general relation of greater and less, without any precise difference or proportion. But when we see the universal exact agreement of all possible sizes of such systems of solids, that they preserve to each other the constant ratio of 3, 2, 1, how beautiful is the theorem, and how are we ravished with its first discovery!

*Easy*
*theorems*

[We may likewise observe that easy or obvious propositions, even where the unity is sufficiently distinct, and determinate, do not please us so much as those which, being less obvious, give us some surprise in the discovery. Thus we find little pleasure in discovering that *A line bisecting the vertical angle of an isosceles triangle, bisects the base,* or the reverse; or that *Equilateral triangles are equiangular.* These truths we almost know intuitively, without demon-

[7] "mind in which we are" – 2nd and 3rd eds.; "mind which we are in" – 1st ed.
[8] Word in brackets added in 4th ed.
[9] "Because however this proposition does contain" – 1st ed.
[10] "with" – 2nd ed.

stration. They are like common goods, or those which men have long possessed, which do not give such sensible joys as much smaller new additions may give us. But let none hence imagine that the sole pleasure of theorems is from surprise; for the same novelty of a single experiment does not please us much, nor ought we to conclude from the greater pleasure accompanying a new or unexpected advantage, that surprise, or novelty is the only pleasure of life, or the only ground of delight in truth.] [11] [Another kind of surprise in certain theorems increases our pleasure above that we have in theorems of greater extent: when we discover a general truth which upon some confused notion we had reputed false, as that *Asymptotes always approaching should never meet the curve.* This is like the joy of unexpected advantage where we dreaded evil. But still the unity of many particulars in the general theorem is necessary to give pleasure in any theorem.] [12]

*Corollaries*    V. [There is another beauty in propositions when one theorem contains a great] [13] multitude of corallaries easily deducible from it. [Thus there are some leading or fundamental properties upon which a long series of theorems can be naturally built. Such a theorem is the 35th of the 1st Book of Euclid, from which the whole art of measuring right-lined areas is deduced by resolution into triangles which are the halves of so many parallelograms, and these are each respectively equal to so many rectangles of the base into the perpendicular altitude. The 47th of the 1st Book is another of like beauty, and so are many others in higher parts of geometry. In the search of nature there is the like beauty in the knowledge of some great principles or universal forces from which innumerable effects do flow. Such is *gravitation* in Sir Isaac Newton's scheme. What is the aim of our ingenious geometers? A continual enlargement of theorems, or making them extensive, showing how what

[11] Passage in brackets added in 2nd ed.
[12] Passage in brackets added in 3rd ed.
[13] "There is another beauty in propositions, which cannot be omitted, which is this, when one theorem shall contain a vast" – 1st ed. "There is another beauty in propositions, which cannot be omitted, which is, when one theorem contains a vast" – 2nd ed.

was formerly known of one figure extends to many others, to figures very unlike the former in appearance.] [14]

It is easy to see how men are charmed with the beauty of such knowledge, besides its usefulness, and how this sets them upon deducing the properties of each figure from one genesis, and demonstrating the mechanic forces from one theorem of the composition of motion, even after they have sufficient knowledge and certainty in all these truths from distinct independent demonstrations. And this pleasure we enjoy even when we have no prospect of obtaining any other advantage from such manner of deduction [than] [15] the immediate pleasure of contemplating the beauty; nor could love of fame excite us to such regular methods of deduction, were we not conscious that mankind are pleased with them immediately, by this *internal sense* of their beauty.

*Fantastic beauty*      It is no less easy to see into what absurd [attempts] [16] men have been led by this sense of beauty, and [an] [17] affectation of obtaining it in the other sciences as well as the mathematics. 'Twas this probably which set Descartes on that hopeful project of deducing all human knowledge from one proposition, viz. *Cogito, ergo sum*; while others [pleaded] [18] that *Impossibile est idem simul esse & non esse* had much fairer pretensions to the style and title of *Principium humanae Cognitionis absolute primum*. Mr. Leibniz had an equal affection for his favourite principle of a *sufficient reason* for everything in nature, and [boasts of the wonders he had wrought in the intellectual world by its

[14] "Thus that theorem which gives us the equation of a curve, whence perhaps most of its properties may be deduced, does some way please and satisfy our mind above any other proposition. Such a theorem also is the 35th of the 1st Book of Euclid, from which the whole art of measuring right-lined areas is deduced by resolution into triangles which are the halves of so many parallelograms, and these are each respectively equal to so many rectangles of the base into the perpendicular altitude. The 47th of the 1st Book is another of like beauty, and so are many others.

"In the search of nature there is the like beauty in the knowledge of some great principles, or universal forces from which innumerable effects do flow. Such is *gravitation* in Sir Isaac Newton's scheme. Such also is the knowledge of the original of *rights, perfect* and *imperfect*, and *external, alienable* and *unalienable*, with their manner of *translation*, from whence the greatest part of moral duties may be deduced in the various relations of human life" – 1st, 2nd, and 3rd eds.

[15] "besides" – 1st ed.
[16] "whimsies" – 1st ed.
[17] "a silly" – 1st and 2nd eds.
[18] "with as little sense contended" – 1st, 2nd, and 3rd eds.

assistance. If we look into particular sciences we see the inconveniences of this love of uniformity. How awkwardly
does Puffendorf deduce the several duties of men to God,
themselves, and their neighbours from his single fundamental
principle of *sociableness to the whole race of mankind*?
This observation is a strong proof that men perceive the
beauty of uniformity in the sciences, since they are led into
unnatural deductions by pursuing it too far.] [19]

VI. This delight which accompanies sciences, or universal
theorems, may really be called a kind of *sensation*, since it
necessarily accompanies the discovery of any proposition,
and is distinct from bare knowledge itself,* being most
violent at first, whereas the knowledge is uniformly the
same. And however knowledge enlarges the mind, and
makes us more capable of comprehensive views, and projects
in some kinds of business when advantage may also arise
to us, yet we may leave it in the breast of every student to
determine whether he has not often felt this pleasure without
such prospect of advantage from the discovery of his theo-

[19] The passage in brackets reads as follows in the 1st ed.: "brags to Dr. Clarke
of the wonders he had wrought in the intellectual world by its assistance; but his
learned antagonist seems to think he had not sufficient reason for his boasting. [See
the letters which passed between Dr. Clarke and Mr. Leibniz, p. 23.] If we look
into particular sciences we may see in the systems learned men have given us of
them the inconveniences of this love of uniformity. [Dr. Cumberland has taken
a great deal of needless pains to reduce the laws of nature to one general principle
and] how awkwardly is Puffendorf forced to deduce the several duties of men to
God, themselves, and their neighbours from his single fundamental principle of
*sociableness to the whole race of mankind*. [As if they had not been better drawn,
each respectively, from their immediate sources, viz. religion, self-love, and
sociableness.] This observation might easily be extended farther, were it necessary, and is a strong proof that men [have a sense of beauty in] uniformity in the
sciences [notwithstanding] the contortions of common sense they are led into by
pursuing it." The first bracketed passage of the above is a footnote which appeared in the 1st, 2nd, and 3rd eds., and was deleted from the 4th. The second and
third bracketed passages were deleted from the 2nd and 3rd eds. The fourth
bracketed passage reads "perceive the beauty of" in 3rd ed. The fifth bracketed
passage reads "even from" in 2nd and 3rd eds.

* Aristotle (*Nicomachean Ethics*, Book 10, Capital 3) justly observes that we
have certain natural propensities to certain actions, or to the exercise of certain
natural powers, without a view to, or intention of obtaining those pleasures which
naturally accompany them. "Also there are many things which we should be
eager to possess if they brought us no pleasure, for instance sight, memory, knowledge, virtue. It may be the case that these things are necessarily attended by
pleasure, but that makes no difference; for we should desire them even if no
pleasure resulted from them." [Hutcheson quotes Aristotle in Greek. The English
translation here supplied is that of H. Rackham.]

rem. All [which] [20] can thence be inferred is only this, that as in our external senses, so in our internal ones, the pleasant sensations generally arise from those objects which calm reason would have recommended, had we understood their use, and which might have engaged our pursuits from self-interest.[21]

*Works of art*    VII. As to the works of art, were we to run through the various artificial contrivances or structures, we should constantly find the foundation of the beauty which appears in them to be some kind of uniformity or unity of proportion among the parts, and of each part to the whole. As there is a [great] [22] diversity of proportions possible, and different kinds of uniformity, so there is room enough for that diversity of fancies observable in architecture, gardening, and such like arts in different nations: they all have uniformity, though the parts in one may differ from those in another. The Chinese or Persian buildings are not like the Grecian and Roman, and yet the former has its uniformity of the various parts to each other, and to the whole, as well as the latter. In that kind of architecture which the Europeans call *regular,* the uniformity of parts is very obvious, the several parts are regular figures, and either equal or similar at least in the same range: the pedestals are parallelopipedons or square prisms; the pillars, cylinders nearly; the arches circu-

[20] "that" – 1st ed.
[21] There follows here, in the 2nd ed., a paragraph deleted from the later editions, although portions of it are included in Section III, Article IV of the 4th ed. It reads, in its entirety, as follows: "If any allege that this pleasure in theorems arises only at first, upon the novelty of the discovery, which occasions surprise, it must be owned indeed that [See Section VI, Article XIII, and the *Spectator* there referred to] novelty is generally very agreeable, and heightens the pleasure in the contemplation of beauty; but then the novelty of a particular truth, found out by measuring, as above mentioned, gives no considerable pleasure, nor surprise. That then which is pleasant and surprising is the first observation of this unity amidst such a great variety. There is indeed another kind of surprise which adds to the beauty of some propositions less universal, and may make them equally pleasant with more universal ones, as when we discover a general truth which seemed before, upon some confused opinion, to be a falsehood: as that *Assymptotes always approaching should never meet the curve.* This is like that joy, which may be very strong and violent, upon the unexpected arrival of a small advantage from that occasion from which we apprehended great evil. But still this unity of many particulars in the general theorem is necessary to make it pleasant." The bracketed passage is a footnote to the above paragraph which appears, like the paragraph, only in the 2nd ed.
[22] "vast" – 1st and 2nd eds.

lar, and all those in the same row equal; there is the same proportion everywhere observed in the same range between the diameters of pillars and their heights, their capitals, the diameters of arches, the heights of the pedestals, the projections of the cornice, and all [the] 23 ornaments in each of our five orders. And though other countries do not follow the Grecian or Roman proportions, yet there is even among them a proportion retained, a uniformity and resemblance of corresponding figures; and every deviation in one part from that proportion which is observed in the rest of the building is displeasing to every eye, and destroys or diminishes at least the beauty of the whole.

VIII. The same might be observed through all other works of art, even to the meanest utensil, the beauty of every one of which we shall always find to have the same foundation of *uniformity amidst variety,* without which [they] 24 appear mean, irregular, and deformed.

## Section IV:

### Of Relative or Comparative Beauty

*Compara-* *tive* *beauty* I. If the preceeding thoughts concerning the foundation of *absolute beauty* be just, we may easily understand wherein *relative beauty* consists. All beauty is relative to the sense of some mind perceiving it; but what we call *relative* is that which is apprehended in any object commonly considered as an *imitation* of some original. And this beauty is founded on a conformity, or a kind of unity between the original and the copy. The original may be either some object in nature, or some established idea; for if there be any known idea as a standard, and rules to fix this image or idea by, we may make a beautiful imitation. Thus a statuary, painter, or poet may please with an Hercules, if his piece retains that grandeur, and those marks of strength and courage which we imagine in that hero.

And farther, to obtain comparative beauty alone, it is not necessary that there be any beauty in the original. The imitation of absolute beauty may indeed in the whole make

23 Word in brackets added in 2nd ed.
24 "they shall" – 1st ed.

a more lovely piece, and yet an exact imitation shall still be beautiful, though the original were entirely void of it. Thus the deformities of old age in a picture, the rudest rocks or mountains in a landscape, if well represented, shall have abundant beauty, though perhaps not so great as if the original were absolutely beautiful, and as well represented. [Nay, perhaps the novelty may make us prefer the representation of irregularity.] [1]

*De-*
*scription*
*in poetry*
II. The same observation holds true in the descriptions of the poets either of natural objects or persons; and this relative beauty is what they should principally endeavour to obtain, as the peculiar beauty of their works. By the *Moratae Fabulae,* or the ἤϑη of Aristotle,[2] we are not to understand virtuous [manners,] [3] but a just representation of manners or characters as they are in nature, and that the actions and sentiments be suited to the characters of the persons to whom they are ascribed in epic and dramatic poetry. Perhaps very good reasons may be suggested from the nature of our passions to prove that a poet should not [draw his characters perfectly virtuous].[4] These characters indeed abstractly considered might give more pleasure, and have more beauty than the imperfect ones which occur in life with a mixture of good and evil; but it may suffice at present to suggest against this choice that we have more lively ideas of imperfect men with all their passions, than of morally perfect heroes such as really never occur to our observation, and of which consequently we cannot judge exactly as to their agreement with the copy. And farther, through consciousness of our own state we are more nearly touched and affected by the imperfect characters, since in them we see represented, in the persons of others, the contrasts of inclinations, and the struggles between the passions of self-love and those of honour and virtue which we often feel in our own breasts. This is the perfection of beauty for which Homer is justly admired, as well as for the variety of his characters.

[1] Passage in brackets added in 3rd ed.
[2] *Poetics* vi. The location in the *Poetics* is given by Scott Elledge in his abridged version of Hutcheson's first *Inquiry: Eighteenth-Century Critical Essays* (Ithaca, New York: Cornell University Press, 1961), vol. 1, p. 552.
[3] "manners in a moral sense" – 1st, 2nd, and 3rd eds.
[4] "out of choice draw the finest characters possible for virtue" – 1st ed.

*Proba-*
*bility,*
*Simile,*
*Metaphor*

III. Many other beauties of poetry may be reduced under this class of *relative beauty*. The *probability* is absolutely necessary to make us imagine *resemblance*. It is by resemblance that *similitudes, metaphors,* and *allegories* are made beautiful, whether either the subject or the thing compared to it have beauty or not; the beauty indeed is greater when both have some original beauty or dignity as well as resemblance, and this is the foundation of the rule of studying *decency* in metaphors and similes as well as likeness. The *measures* and *cadence* are instances of harmony, and come under the head of absolute beauty.

*Proneness*
*to*
*compare*

IV. We may here observe a strange proneness in our minds to make perpetual comparisons of all things which occur to our observation, even of those which [are very different from each other.] [5] There are certain resemblances in the motions of all animals upon like passions, which easily found a comparison; but this does not serve to entertain our fancy. Inanimate objects have often such positions as resemble those of the human body in various circumstances. These airs or gestures of the body are indications of [certain] [6] dispositions in the mind, so that our very passions and affections, as well as other circumstances, obtain a resemblance to natural inanimate objects. Thus a tempest at sea is often an emblem of wrath; a plant or tree drooping under the rain of a person in sorrow; a poppy bending its stalk, or a flower withering when cut by the plow resembles the death of a blooming hero; an aged oak in the mountains shall represent an old empire; a flame seizing a wood shall represent a war. In short, everything in nature, by our strange inclination to resemblance, shall be brought to represent other things, even the most remote, especially the passions and circumstances of human nature in which we are more nearly concerned; and to confirm this and furnish instances of it one need only look into Homer or Virgil. A fruitful fancy would find in a grove, or a wood an emblem for every character in a commonwealth, and every turn of temper or station in life.

*Intention*

V. Concerning that kind of comparative beauty which has

[5] "would seem very remote" – 1st and 2nd eds.
[6] Word in brackets added in 2nd ed.

a necessary relation to some established idea, we may observe that some works of art acquire a distinct beauty by their correspondence to some universally supposed intention in the artificers, or the persons who employed him. And to obtain this beauty sometimes they do not form their works so as to attain the highest perfection of original beauty separately considered, because a composition of this relative beauty, along with some degree of the original kind, may give more pleasure than a more perfect original beauty separately. Thus we see that strict regularity in laying out of gardens in parterres, vistas, parallel walks, is often neglected to obtain an imitation of nature even in some of its wildness. And we are more pleased with this imitation, especially when the scene is large and spacious, than with the more confined exactness of regular works. So likewise in the monuments erected in honour of deceased heroes, although a cylinder, or prism, or regular solid may have more original beauty than a very acute pyramid or obelisk, yet the latter pleases more by answering better to supposed intentions of stability and being conspicuous. For the same reason, cubes or square prisms are generally chosen for the pedestals of statues, and not any of the more beautiful solids, which do not seem so secure from rolling. This may be the reason too why columns or pillars look best when made a little taper from the middle, or a third from the bottom, that they may not seem top-heavy and in danger of falling.

VI. The like reason may influence artists in many other instances to depart from the rules of original beauty as above laid down. And yet this is no argument against our sense of beauty being founded, as was above explained, on uniformity amidst variety, but only an evidence that our sense of beauty of the original kind may be varied and overbalanced by another kind of beauty.

VII. This beauty arising from correspondence to intention would open to curious observers a new scene of beauty in the works of nature, by considering how the mechanism of the various parts known to us seems adapted to the perfection of that part, and yet in subordination to the good of some system or whole. We generally suppose the good of the greatest whole, or of all beings, to have been the intention of the Author of nature, and cannot avoid being pleased when we see any part of this design executed in the systems we are acquainted with. The observations already made on this subject are in everyone's hand, in the treatise of our late improvers of *mechanical philosophy*. We [shall only observe here that everyone has a certain pleasure in] [7] seeing any design well executed by curious mechanism, even when his own advantage is no way concerned, [and also] [8] in discovering the design to which any complex machine is adapted, when he has perhaps had a general knowledge of the machine before, without seeing its correspondence or aptness to execute any design.*[9]

---

[7] "may only here observe the pleasure which anyone shall receive from" – 1st ed.

[8] "as also that pleasant sensation he shall have" – 1st ed.

* 'Tis surprising to see the ingenious author of *Alciphron* alleging that all beauty observed is solely some *use* perceived or imagined, for no other reason than this, that the apprehension of the use intended occurs continually when we are judging of the forms of chairs, doors, tables, and some other things of obvious use, and that we like those forms most which are fittest for the use. Whereas we see that in these very things *similitude* of parts is regarded, where unlike parts would be equally useful. Thus the feet of a chair would be of the same use, though unlike, were they equally long; though one were straight and the other bended; or one bending outwards and the other inwards. A coffin-shape for a door would bear a more manifest aptitude to the human shape than that which artists require. And then what is the use of these imitations of nature, or of its works, in architecture? Why should a pillar please which has some of the human proportions? Is the *end* or *use* of a pillar the same as of a man? Why the imitation of other natural or well-proportioned things in the entablature? Is there then a *sense of imitation* relishing it where there is no other use than this, that it naturally pleases? Again, is no man pleased with the shapes of any animals but those which he expects use from? The shapes of the horse or the ox promise use to the owner. But is he the only person who relishes the beauty? And is there no beauty discerned in plants, in flowers, in animals, whose use is to us unknown? But what is still more surprising is his representing Aristotle as giving the ἐπαιμετὸν, for the notion of the καλὸν when he has often told us that the καλὸν is prior to it; that we love praise from others as it gives testimony to, and confirms our opinion of, our being possessed of virtue, or the καλὸν; and that the superior excellency of this, which we antecedently perceive, is the reason why we love praise. See *Nicomachean Ethics*, Book 1, Capital 5, and often elsewhere. 'Tis true that the καλὸν is laudable and, as Plato asserts, all-wise, ἡδὺ, χαἰῷφέλιμιν, at last, and so does everyone maintain who asserts a moral sense, in that very assertion. And yet the Doctor has found out the art of making this an objection to a moral sense.

[9] Footnote added in 4th ed. It was an answer to certain criticisms of the moral sense, and the sense of beauty, which Bishop Berkeley had advanced in the Third Dialogue of his *Alciphron, or the Minute Philosopher* (1732). The passage in Book I of Aristotle's *Nicomachean Ethics* to which Hutcheson refers seems to be the following: "Moreover men's motive in pursuing honour seems to be to assure themselves of their own merit; at least they seek to be honoured by men of judgement and by people who know them, that is, they desire to be honoured on the ground of virtue. It is clear therefore that in the opinion at all events of men

The arguments by which we prove reason and design in any cause from the beauty of the effects are so frequently used in some of the highest subjects that it may be necessary to inquire a little more particularly into them, to see how far they will hold, and with what degree of evidence.

## Section V:

### *Concerning our Reasonings about Design and Wisdom in the Cause, from the Beauty or Regularity of Effects*

*Sense, arbitrary in its Author*

I. There seems to be no necessary connection of our pleasing ideas of beauty with the uniformity or regularity of the objects, from the nature of things, antecedent to some constitution of the Author of our nature, which has made such forms pleasant to us. Other minds may be so framed as to receive no pleasure from uniformity, and we actually find that the same regular forms [seem not] [1] equally to please all the animals known to us, as shall probably appear [hereafter.] [2] Therefore let us make what is the most unfavourable supposition to the present argument, [viz.] [3] that the constitution of our sense so as to approve uniformity is merely arbitrary in the Author of our nature, and that there are an infinity of tastes or relishes of beauty possible, so that it would be impossible to throw together fifty or a hundred pebbles which should not make an agreeable habitation for some animal or other, and appear beautiful to it. And then it is plain that from the perception of beauty in any one effect we should have no reason to conclude design in the cause; for a sense might be so constituted as to be pleased with such irregularity as may be the effect of an undirected force.* But then, as there are an infinity of forms possible

of action, virtue is a greater good than honour; and one might perhaps accordingly suppose that virtue rather than honour is the end of the Political Life." (1096a; trans. H. Rackham.)

  [1] "do not seem" – 1st ed.
  [2] "afterwards" – 1st and 2nd eds.
  [3] "possible" – 1st ed.
  * By *undirected force*, or *undesigning force*, is to be understood that force with which an agent may put matter into motion without having any design or intention to produce any particular form. The *Conatus ad motum*, without an actual line of direction, seems such a gross absurdity in the Cartesian scheme that it is below [our notice.] But men have so many confused notions of some nature, or chance impressing motions without any design or intention of producing any

into which any system may be reduced, an infinity of places in which animals may be situated, and an infinity of relishes or senses [in these animals] [4] is supposed possible, that in the immense spaces any one animal should by chance be placed in a system agreeable to its taste must be improbable as infinite to one at least. And much more unreasonable is it to expect from chance that a multitude of animals agreeing in their sense of beauty should obtain agreeable places.

*Undirected force*    II. [There is also] [5] the same probability that in any one system of matter an undirected force will produce a regular form as any one given irregular one. But still the irregular forms into which any system may be ranged surpass in multitude the regular as infinite does unity; for what holds in one small system will hold in a thousand, a million, a universe, with more advantage, viz. that the irregular forms possible infinitely surpass the regular. For instance, the area of an inch square is capable of an infinity of regular forms, the equilateral triangle, the square, the pentagon, hexagon, heptagon, etc.; but for each one regular form there are an infinity of irregular, as an infinity of scalena for the one equilateral triangle, an infinity of trapezia for the one square, of irregular pentagons for the one regular, and so on. And therefore supposing any one system agitated by undesigned force, it [is] [6] infinitely more probable that it will resolve itself into an irregular form than a regular. Thus, that a

particular effect, that it may be useful to show that even this very absurd *postulatum*, though it were granted them, is insufficient to answer the appearances in the regularity of the world; and this is what is attempted in the first fourteen articles of this section. These arguments would really be useless if all men were persuaded of what to a man of just thought will appear pretty obvious, that there can be no thought-less agent, and that *chance* and *nature* are mere empty names, as they are used on this occasion relative only to our ignorance. [Words in brackets read "the dignity of common sense to vouchsafe to confute it" in 2nd and 3rd eds. This footnote was completely rewritten and expanded in the 2nd ed. It reads as follows in the 1st ed.: "This expression is taken from the Cartesian scheme in which the Author of nature is supposed to have designedly impressed a general force or *Conatus ad motum* upon the mass of matter, without any direction whatsoever. This nonsensical notion did so much prevail, and men have so many confused conceptions of nature and chance, as real beings operating without wisdom or design, that it may be useful to show that their very absurd *postulatum* is wholly insufficient, though it were granted them, to answer the appearances in the regularity of the world. And this is what is attempted in the first fourteen articles of this section."]

[4] Words in brackets added in 2nd ed.
[5] "It is also certain that there is" – 1st ed.
[6] "shall be" – 1st ed.

system of six parts upon agitation shall not obtain the form of a regular hexagon is at least infinite to unity; and the more complex we make the system, the greater is the hazard, from a very obvious reason.

We see this confirmed by our constant experience, that regularity never arises from any undesigned force of ours; and from this we conclude that wherever there is any regularity in the disposition of a system capable of many other dispositions, there must have been design in the cause; and the force of this evidence increases according to the multiplicity of parts employed.

But this conclusion is too rash unless some farther proof be introduced, and what leads us into it is this. Men who have a sense of beauty in regularity are led generally in all their arrangements of bodies to study some kind of regularity, and seldom ever design irregularity: [hence] [7] we judge the same of other beings too, [viz.] [8] that they study regularity, and presume upon intention in the cause wherever we see it, making irregularity always a presumption of want of design, whereas [if other agents have different senses of beauty,] [9] or if they have no sense of it at all, irregularity may as well be designed as regularity. And then let it be observed that in this case there is just the same reason to conclude design in the cause from any one irregular effect as from a regular one. For since there are an infinity of other forms possible as well as this irregular one produced, and since to such a being * [10] void of a sense of beauty, all forms are as to its own relish indifferent, and all agitated matter meeting must make some form or other, and all

[7] "and hence" – 1st ed.
[8] Word in brackets added in 2nd ed.
[9] "if different senses of beauty be in other agents" – 1st ed.
* There is a great difference between such a being as is here mentioned and a being which has no intention for any reason whatsoever to produce one form more than another. This latter sort of being, as to the present argument, would be the same with chance, but not the former. For though a being has no sense of beauty, he may notwithstanding be capable of design, and of intention in the cause, even where the cause is supposed to have no sense of beauty in such forms, since perhaps he may have other reasons moving him to choose such forms. Thus supposing the Deity [not immediately] pleased with regularity, uniformity, or similarity in bodies, yet there may be reasons moving him to produce such objects, such as the pleasing his creatures, having given them a sense of beauty founded on these qualities. See the last paragraphs of the last Section.
[10] Bracketed words in footnote read "no way necessarily" in 1st and 2nd eds.

forms, upon supposition that the force is applied by an agent void of a sense of beauty, would equally prove design, it is plain that no one form proves it more than another, or can prove it at all, except from a general metaphysical consideration, [that] [11] there is no proper agent without design and intention, and that every effect flows from the intention of some cause.

*Similar forms by chance, impossible*
III. This however follows from the above [mentioned] [12] considerations, that supposing a mass of matter surpassing a cubic inch as infinite of the first power does unity, and that this whole mass were some way determined from its own nature without any design in a cause (which perhaps is scarce possible) to resolve itself into [parts whose solid contents were each a cubic inch],[13] and into a prismatic form whose base should always be $\frac{1}{2}$ of a square inch – suppose these conditions determined, and all others left to undirected force, all [which] [14] we could expect from undirected force in this case would be one equilateral prism, or two perhaps, because there are an infinity of irregular prisms possible of the same base and solid content; and when we [met] [15] with many such prisms, we must probably conclude [them produced by design],[16] since they are more than could have been expected by the laws of hazard.

IV. But if this infinite mass was [not] [17] determined to a prismatic form, [we could only expect from its casual concourse one prism of any kind, since there is an infinity of other solids into which the mass might be resolved; and if we found any great number of prisms, we should have reason to presume design.] [18] So that in a mass of matter as infinite of the first power, we could not from any concourse

---

[11] "too subtle to be certain, that" – 1st and 2nd eds.

[12] "offered" – 1st ed.

[13] "the solid content of a cubic inch" – 2nd ed.; "cubic inches solid content" – 1st ed.

[14] "that" – 1st ed.

[15] "meet" – 1st ed.

[16] "design as producing them" – 1st ed.

[17] "no way" – 1st and 2nd eds.

[18] "since there are an infinity of other forms possible, we could only expect from the casual concourse of such a mass as was supposed in the last case, one prism of any kind, since there are an infinity of other solids possible into which the mass might be resolved; and if we found any great number of prisms, we should have presumption of design" – 1st ed.

or agitation expect with any good ground a body of any given form, since of any dimension there are infinite forms possible, and of any form there are an infinity of dimensions; and if we found several bodies of the same dimension and form, we should have so much presumption for design.

V. There is one trifling objection which may perhaps arise from the crystalizing of certain bodies, when the fluid is evaporated in which they were swimming: for in this we frequently see regular forms arising, though there is nothing [supposed in this affair but an undirected force of attraction.] [19] But to remove this objection we need only consider that we have good reason to believe that the smallest particles of crystalized bodies have fixed regular forms given them in the constitution of nature; and then it is easy to conceive how their attraction may produce regular forms. But unless we suppose some preceding regularity in the figures of attracting bodies, they [can] [20] never form any regular body at all. And hence we see how improbable it is that the whole mass of matter, not only in this globe but in all the fixed stars known to us by our eyes or glasses, were they a thousand times larger than our astronomers suppose, could in any concourse have produced any number of similar bodies regular or irregular.

*Combi-*
*nations*
*by chance,*
*impossible*

VI. And let it be here observed that there are many compositions of bodies which the smallest degree of design could easily effect, which yet we would in vain expect from all the powers of chance or undesigned force, [after] [21] an infinity of rencounters, even supposing a dissolution of every form except the regular one, that the parts might be prepared for a new agitation. Thus, supposing we could expect one equilateral prism of any given dimensions should be formed from undirected force, in an infinity of matter some way determined to resolve itself into bodies of a given solid content (which is all we could expect, since it is infinite to one after the solid content is obtained that the body shall not be prismatical, and allowing it prismatical, it is infinite to one that it shall not be equilateral); and, again, supposing another infinity of matter determined to resolve itself into

[19] "in this affair but an undirected force of attraction supposed" – 1st ed.
[20] "shall" – 1st ed.
[21] "even after" – 1st ed.

tubes of orifices exactly equal to the bases of the former prisms, it is again at least as the second power of infinite to unity that not one of these tubes shall be both prismatic and equiangular. And then if the tube were thus formed, so as to be exactly capable of receiving one of the prisms and no more, it is infinite to one that they shall never meet in infinite space; and should they meet, it is infinite to one that the axes of the prism and tube shall never happen in the same straight line; and supposing they did, it is again as infinite to three that angle shall not meet angle, so as to enter. We see then how infinitely improbable it is that all the powers of chance in infinite matter, agitated through infinite ages, could ever effect this small composition of a prism entering a prismatic bore, and that all our hazard for it would at most be but as three is to the third power of infinite. And yet the smallest design could easily effect it.

VII. May we not then justly count it altogether absurd, and next to an absolute strict impossibility, that all the powers of undirected force should ever effect such a complex machine as the most imperfect plant, or the meanest animal, even in one instance? For the improbability just increases as the complication of mechanism in these natural bodies surpasses that simple combination above mentioned.

VIII. Let it be here observed that the preceding reasoning from the frequency of regular bodies of one form in the universe, and from the combinations of various bodies, is entirely independent on any perception of beauty, and would equally prove design in the cause although there were no being which perceived beauty in any form whatsoever; for it is, in short, this: *that the recurring of any effect oftener than the laws of hazard determine, gives presumption of design; and, that combinations which no undesigned force could give us reason to expect must necessarily prove the same; and, that with superior probability, as the multitude of cases in which the contrary [might]* [22] *happen, surpasses all the cases in which this could happen* – which appears to be in the simplest cases at least as infinite does [to] [23] unity. And the frequency of similar irregular forms, or exact

<hr>

[22] "might possibly" – 1st ed.
[23] Word in brackets added in 4th ed.

combinations of them, is an equal argument of design in the cause, since the similarity, or exact combinations of irregular forms, are as little to be expected from all the powers of undirected force as any sort whatsoever.

IX. To bring this nearer to something like a theorem, although the idea of infinite be troublesome enough to manage in reasoning, the powers of chance, with infinite matter in infinite ages, may answer hazards as the fifth power of infinite and no more; thus the quantity of matter may be conceived as the third power of infinite and no more, the various degrees of force may make another power of infinite, and the number of rencounters may make the fifth. But this last only holds on supposition that after every rencounter there is no cohesion, but all is dissolved again for a new concourse, except in similar forms or exact combinations, which supposition is entirely groundless, since we see dissimilar bodies cohering as strongly as any, and rude masses more than any combinations. Now to produce any given body, in a given place or situation, and of given dimensions, or shape, the hazards of the contrary are one power of infinite at least to obtain the place or situation; when the situation is obtained, the solid content requires another power of infinite to obtain it; the situation and solidity obtained require for accomplishing the simplest given shape at least the other three powers of infinite. For instance, let the shape be a four-sided prism or parallelopiped. That the surfaces should be planes requires one power; that they should be parallel in this case, or inclined in any given angle in any other case, requires another power of infinite; and that they should be in any given ratio to each other requires at least the third power. For in each of these heads there [is still an infinity at least] [24] of other cases possible beside the one given. So that all the powers of chance could only produce perhaps *one* body of every simpler shape or size at most, and this is all we could expect. We might expect one pyramid, or cube, or prism perhaps; but when we increase the conditions required, the prospect must grow more improbable, as in more complex figures, and in all combinations of bodies, and in similar species,

[24] "are at least still an infinity" – 1st ed.

which we never could reasonably hope from chance; and therefore where we see them we must certainly ascribe them to design.

*Combi-*
*nations of*
*irregular*
*forms,*
*equally*
*impossible*

X. The combinations of regular forms, or of irregular ones exactly adapted to each other, require such vast powers of infinite to effect them, and the hazards of the contrary forms are so infinitely numerous, that all probability or possibility of their being accomplished by chance seems quite to vanish. Let us apply the cases in Article VI [in] [25] this Section about the prism and tube to our simplest machines, such as a pair of wheels of our ordinary carriages: each circular, spokes equal in length, thickness, shape; the wheels set parallel, the axle-tree fixed in the nave of both, and secured from coming out at either end. Now the cases in which the contrary might have happened from undirected concourses, were there no more required than what is just now mentioned, must amount in multitude to a power of infinite equal to every circumstance required. What shall we say then of a plant, a tree, an animal, a man, with such multitudes of adapted vessels, such articulations, insertions of muscles, diffusion of veins, arteries, nerves? The improbability that such machines [arising daily in such numbers in all parts of the earth with such similarity of structure should be the effect of chance is beyond all conception or expression.] [26]

XI. Further, were all the former reasoning from similarity of forms and combinations groundless, and could chance give us ground to expect such forms, with exact combination, yet we could only promise [ourselves] [27] *one* of these forms among an *infinity* of others. When we see then such a *multitude* of individuals of a species, similar to each other in a [great] [28] number of parts, and when we see in each individual the corresponding members so exactly [like] [29] each other, what possible room is there left for questioning design in the universe? None but the barest possibility against an

[25] "of" – 1st, 2nd, and 3rd eds.
[26] "should be the effect of chance must be near the infinitesimal power of infinite to unity" – 1st, 2nd, and 3rd eds.
[27] Word in brackets added in 2nd ed.
[28] "vast" – 1st and 2nd eds.
[29] "like to" – 1st ed.

inconceivably great probability, surpassing everything which is not strict demonstration.

XII. This argument, as [has] [30] been already observed,* is quite abstracted from any sense of beauty in any particular form. For the exact similarity of a hundred or a thousand trapezia proves design as well as the similarity of squares, since both are equally above the powers of undirected force or [chance]; [31] and what is above the powers of chance must give us proportionable presumption for design.

Thus, allowing that a leg or arm or eye might have been the effect of chance (which was shown to be most absurd and next to absolutely impossible), that it [should] [32] not have a corresponding leg, arm, eye, exactly similar, must be a hazard of a power of infinite proportioned to the complication of parts; for in proportion to this is the multitude of cases increased in which it would not have a corresponding member similar. So that allowing twenty or thirty parts in such a structure, it would be as the twentieth or thirtieth power of infinite to unity that the corresponding part should not be similar. What shall we say then of the similar forms of a whole species?

*Gross similarity by chance, impossible*    XIII. If it be objected that natural bodies are not exactly similar, but only grossly so to our senses, as that a vein, an artery, a bone is not perhaps exactly similar to its correspondent in the same animal, though it appears so to our senses, which judge only of the bulk, and do not discern the small constituent parts; and that in the several individuals of a species the dissimilarity is always sensible, often in the internal structure, and [always] [33] in the external appearance: to remove this objection it will be sufficient to show that the multitude of cases [wherein] [34] sensible dissimilitude could have happened are still infinitely more than all the cases in which sensible similitude might [be retained], [35] so that the same reasoning holds from sensible similarity as from the

---

[30] "it has" – 1st ed.
* See above, Article VIII.
[31] "chance, as the hundredth or thousandth power of infinite surpasses unity" – 1st, 2nd, and 3rd eds.
[32] "would" – 2nd ed.
[33] "often, nay always" – 1st and 2nd eds.
[34] "where" – 1st and 2nd eds.
[35] Words in brackets added in 3rd ed.

mathematically exact; and again that the cases of gross dissimilarity do in the same manner surpass the cases of gross similarity as infinite does one.

XIV. To prove both these assertions let us consider a simple instance. [Suppose] [36] a trapezium of a foot square in area [should] [37] appear grossly similar to another, while no one side differs by 1/10 of an inch, or no angle in one surpasses the corresponding one in the other above ten [minutes].[38] Now this tenth of an inch is infinitely divisible, [as are also] [39] the ten minutes, so that the cases of insensible dissimilarity under apparent similarity are really infinite. But then it is also plain that there are an infinity of different sensibly dissimilar trapezia, even of the same area, according as we vary a side by one tenth, two tenths, three tenths, and so on, and [vary] [40] the angles and another side so as to keep the area equal. Now in each of these infinite degrees of sensible dissimilitude the several tenths are infinitely divisible as well as in the first case, so that the multitude of sensible dissimilarities are to the multitude of insensible dissimilarities under apparent resemblance, still as the second power of infinite to the first, or as infinite to unity. And then how vastly greater must the multitude be of all possible sensible dissimilarities in such complex bodies as legs, arms, eyes, arteries, veins, skeletons?

XV. As to the dissimilarities of animals of the same species, it is in the same manner plain that the possible cases of gross dissimilarity are infinite, and then every case of gross dissimilarity contains also all the cases of insensible dissimilarity. Thus, if we could count all animals of a species grossly similar, while there was no limb which in length or diameter did exceed the ordinary shape by above a third of the head, it is plain that there are an infinity of [sensibly different gross] [41] dissimilarities possible, and then in each of these cases of gross dissimilarity there are an infinity of cases of nicer dissimilarity, since 1/3 of the head may be

---

[36] Word in brackets added in 2nd ed.
[37] "shall" – 1st ed.
[38] "minutes perhaps" – 1st ed.
[39] "as also are" – 1st ed.
[40] "varying" – 1st ed.
[41] "gross" – 1st and 2nd eds.

infinitely divided. To take a low but easy instance, two cockle-shells which fitted each other naturally may have an infinity of insensible differences, but still there are an infinity of possible sensible differences; and then in any one of the sensibly different forms there may be the same infinity of insensible differences beside the sensible one. So that still the hazard for even gross similarity from chance is infinite to one, and this always increases by a power of infinite for every distinct member of the animal in which even gross similarity is retained, since the addition of every member or part to a complex machine makes a new infinity of cases in which sensible dissimilarity may happen; and this infinity combined with the infinite cases of the former parts raises the hazard by a power of infinite.

Now this may sufficiently show us the absurdity of the Cartesian or Epicurean hypothesis, even granting their postulation of undirected force impressed on infinite matter, and seems almost a demonstration of design in the universe.

[XVI. One objection more remains to be removed, viz. that some imagine this argument may hold better *a priori* than *a posteriori*; that is, we have better reason to believe, when we see a cause about to act, without knowledge, that he will not attain any given or desired end; than we have, on the other hand, to believe, when we see the end actually attained, that he acted with knowledge. Thus, say they, when a particular person is about to draw a ticket in a lottery, where there is but one prize to a thousand blanks, it is highly probable that he shall draw a blank. But suppose we have seen him actually draw for himself the prize, we have no ground to conclude that he had knowledge or art to accomplish this end. But the answer is obvious. In such contrivances we generally have, from the circumstances of the lottery, very strong moral arguments which almost demonstrate that art can have no place; so that a probability of a thousand to one (may) [42] not surmount those arguments. But let the probability be increased, and it will soon surmount all arguments to the contrary. For instance, if we saw a man ten times successively draw prizes in a lottery where there were but ten prizes to ten thousand blanks, I fancy few would

[42] "does" – 2nd ed.

question whether he used art or not; much less would we imagine it were chance, if we saw a man draw for his own gain successively a hundred, or a thousand prizes from among a proportionably greater number of blanks. Now in the works of nature the case is entirely different: we have not the least argument against art or design. An intelligent cause is surely at least as probable a notion as *Chance, General Force, Conatus ad Motum*, or the *Clinamen Principiorum*, to account for any effect whatsoever. And then all the regularity, combinations, similarities of species, are so many demonstrations that there was design and intelligence in the cause of this universe; whereas in fair lotteries all art in drawing is made, if not actually impossible, at least highly improbable.] [43]

*Irregu-larity does not prove want of design*   XVII. Let it be here observed also that a rational agent may be capable of impressing a force [without] [44] intending to produce any particular form, and of designedly producing irregular or dissimilar forms, as well as regular and similar. And hence it follows that although all the regularity, combination, and similarity in the universe are presumptions of design, yet irregularity is no presumption of the contrary, unless we suppose that the agent is determined from a sense of beauty always to act regularly, and delight in similarity, and that he can have no other inconsistent motive of action – which last is plainly absurd. We do not want in the universe many effects which seem to have been left to the general laws of motion upon some great impulse, and have many instances where similarity has been [plainly designed] [45] in some respects, and probably neglected in others, or even dissimilarity designed. Thus we see the general exact resemblance between the two eyes of most persons; and yet perhaps no other third eye in the world is exactly like them. We see a gross conformity of shape in all persons in innumerable parts, and yet no two individuals of any species are undistinguishable, which perhaps is intended for valuable purposes to the whole species.

*Wisdom, Prudence*   XVIII. Hitherto the proof amounts only to *design* or *intention* barely, in opposition to *blind force* or *chance*; and

[43] Paragraph in brackets added in 2nd ed.
[44] "when he is not" – 1st ed.
[45] "designed plainly" – 1st ed.

we see the proof of this is independent on the arbitrary constitution of our internal sense of beauty. Beauty is often supposed an argument of more than design, to wit, wisdom and prudence in the cause. Let us inquire also into this.

*Wisdom* denotes *the pursuing of the best ends by the best means*; and therefore before we can from any effect prove the cause to be wise we must know what is best to the cause or agent. Among men who have pleasure in contemplating uniformity, the beauty of effects is an argument of wisdom, because this is good to them; but the same argument would not hold as to a being void of this sense of beauty. And therefore the beauty apparent to us in nature will not of itself prove wisdom in the cause, unless this cause, or Author of Nature, be supposed benevolent; and then indeed the happiness of mankind is desirable or good to the Supreme Cause, and that form which pleases us is an argument of his wisdom. And the strength of this argument is always in proportion to the degree of beauty produced in nature, and exposed to the view of any rational agent, since upon supposition of a benevolent Deity all apparent beauty produced is an evidence of the execution of a benevolent design to give [them] [46] the pleasures of beauty.

But what more immediately proves wisdom is this: when we see any machine with a great complication of parts actually obtaining an end we justly conclude that since this could not have been the effect of chance, it must have been intended for that end, which is obtained by it. And then the ends or intentions, being in part known, the complication of organs, and their nice disposition adapted to this end, is an evidence of a comprehensive large understanding in the cause, according to the multiplicity of parts, and the appositeness of their structure, even when we do not know the intention of the whole.

*General causes*  XIX. [There is another kind of beauty from which we conclude wisdom in the cause, as well as design],[47] *when we see many useful or beautiful effects flowing from one general cause.* There is a very good reason for this conclusion among

---

[46] "him" – 1st and 2nd eds.

[47] "There is another kind of beauty also which is still pleasing to our sense, and from which we conclude wisdom in the cause as well as design, and that is" – 1st and 2nd eds.

men. Interest must lead beings of limited powers, who are uncapable of a great diversity of operations, and distracted by them, to choose this frugal economy of their forces, and to look upon such management as an evidence of wisdom in other beings like themselves. Nor is this speculative reason all which influences them, for even beside this consideration of interest they are determined by a sense of beauty where that reason does not hold, as when we are judging of the productions of other agents about whose economy we are not sollicitous. Thus, who does not approve of it as a perfection in clock-work that three or four motions of the hour, minute, and second hands, and monthly plate, should arise from one spring or weight, rather than from three, or four springs, or weights, in a very compound machine, which should perform the same effects, and answer all the same purposes with equal exactness? Now the foundation of this beauty plainly appears to be [an] [48] uniformity, or unity of cause amidst diversity of effects.

*General laws*     XX. [We shall * hereafter offer some reasons why the Author of nature may] [49] choose to operate in this manner by general laws and universal extensive causes, although the reason just now mentioned does not hold with an almighty being. This is certain, that we have some of the most delightful instances of universal causes in the works of nature, and that the most studious men in these subjects are so delighted with the observation of them that they always look upon them as evidences of wisdom in the administration of nature, from a sense of beauty.

XXI. The wonderfully simple mechanism which performs all animal motions was mentioned ** already; nor is that of the inanimate parts of nature less admirable. How innumerable are the effects of that one principle of heat derived to us from the sun, which is not only delightful to our sight and feeling, and the means of discerning objects, but is the cause of rains, springs, rivers, winds, and the universal cause of vegetation! The uniform principle of gravity preserves

[48] Word in brackets added in 4th ed.
* See the last Section.
[49] "We may perhaps afterwards offer some reasons why the Author of nature may perhaps" – 1st ed.
** See above, Section II, Article VIII.

at once the planets in their orbits, gives cohesion to the parts of each globe, and stability to mountains, hills, and artificial structures. It raises the sea in tides, and sinks them again, and restrains them in their channels. It drains the earth of its superfluous moisture by rivers. It raises vapours by its influence on the air, and brings them down again in rains. It gives an uniform pressure to our atmosphere, necessary to our bodies in general, and more especially to our inspiration in breathing, and furnishes us with an universal movement, capable of being applied in innumerable engines. How incomparably more beautiful is this structure than if we supposed so many distinct volitions in the Deity, producing every particular effect, and preventing some of the accidental evils which casually flow from the general law! [We may rashly imagine that] [50] this latter manner of operation might have been more useful to us, and it would have been no distraction to omnipotence; but then the great beauty had been lost, and there had been no more pleasure in the contemplation of this scene, which is now so delightful. One would rather choose to run the hazard of its casual evils, than part with that harmonious form which has been an unexhausted source of delight to the successive spectators in all ages.

*Miracles*    XXII. Hence we see that however miracles may prove the superintendency of a voluntary agent, and that the universe is not guided by necessity or fate, yet that mind must be weak and inadvertent which needs them to confirm the belief of a wise and good Deity, since the deviation from general laws, unless upon very extraordinary occasions, must be a presumption of inconstancy and weakness, rather than of steady wisdom and power, and must weaken the best arguments we can have for the sagacity and power of the universal mind.

[50] "And yet" – 1st ed.

Section VI:

*Of the Universality of the Sense of Beauty Among Men*

*Internal sense not an immediate source of pain*
I. We before * insinuated that all beauty has a relation to some perceiving power. And, consequently, since we know not [how great a] [1] variety of senses [there] [2] may be among animals, there is no form in nature concerning which we can pronounce that it has no beauty; for it may still please some perceiving power. But our *Inquiry* is confined to men; and before we examine the *universality* of this sense of beauty, or their agreement in approving uniformity, it may be proper to consider [whether,] [3] as the other senses which give us pleasure do also give us pain, so this sense of beauty does make some objects disagreeable to us, and the occasion of pain.

That many objects give no pleasure to our sense is obvious: many are certainly void of beauty. But then there is no form which seems necessarily disagreeable of itself, when we dread no other evil from it, and compare it with nothing better of the kind. Many objects are naturally displeasing, and distasteful to our external senses, as well as others pleasing and agreeable, as smells, tastes, and some separate sounds; but as to our sense of beauty, no composition of objects which give not unpleasant simple ideas, seems positively unpleasant or painful of itself, had we never observed anything better of the kind. Deformity is only the absence of beauty, or deficiency in the beauty expected in any species. Thus bad music pleases rustics who never heard any better, and the finest ear is not offended with tuning of instruments if it be not too tedious, where no harmony is expected; and yet much smaller dissonancy shall offend amidst the performance, where harmony is expected. A rude heap of stones is no way offensive to one who shall be displeased with irregularity in architecture, where beauty was expected. And had there been a species of that form which we [now call] [4] ugly or deformed, and had we never seen or expected greater

---

* See above, Section I, Article XVII; Section IV, Article I.
[1] "the" – 1st ed.
[2] "which" – 1st ed.
[3] "if" – 1st ed.
[4] "call now" – 1st and 2nd eds.

beauty, we should have received no disgust from it, although the pleasure would not have been so great in this form as in those we now admire. Our sense of beauty seems designed to give us positive pleasure, but not positive pain or disgust, any farther than what arises from disappointment.

*Appro-*
*bation*
*and dislike*
*from*
*associ-*
*ations*
*of ideas*

II. There are indeed many faces which at first view are apt to raise dislike; but this is generally not from any deformity which of itself is positively displeasing, but either from want of expected beauty, or much more from their carrying some natural indications of morally bad dispositions, which we all acquire a faculty of discerning in countenances, airs, and gestures. That this is not occasioned by any form positively disgusting will appear from this, that if upon long acquaintance we are sure of finding sweetness of temper, humanity, and cheerfulness, although the bodily form continues, it shall give us no disgust or displeasure; whereas [if anything were] [5] naturally disagreeable, or the occasion of pain, or positive distaste, it would always continue so, even although the aversion we might have toward it were counterbalanced by other considerations. There are horrors raised by some objects, which are only the effect of fear of ourselves, or compassion towards others, when either reason, or some foolish association of ideas, makes us apprehend danger, and not the effect of anything in the form itself; for we find that most of [those] [6] objects which excite horror at first, when experience or reason has removed the fear, may become the occasions of pleasure, [as] [7] ravenous beasts, a tempestuous sea, a craggy precipice, a dark shady valley.

*Associ-*
*ations*

III. We shall see * hereafter that associations of ideas make objects pleasant and delightful which are not naturally apt to give any such pleasures; and the same way, the casual conjunctions of ideas may give a disgust where there is nothing disagreeable in the form itself. And this is the occasion of many fantastic aversions to figures of some animals, and to some other forms. Thus swine, serpents of all kinds, and some insects really beautiful enough, are

[5] "what were" – 1st ed.; "if anything was" – 2nd ed.
[6] "these" – 1st ed.
[7] "as in" – 1st ed.
* See below, Articles XII, XIII, of this Section.

beheld with aversion by many people who have got some accidental ideas associated to them. And for distastes of this kind no other account can be given.

*Universality of this sense*

IV. But as to the universal agreement of mankind in their sense of beauty from uniformity amidst variety, we must consult experience. And as we allow all men reason, since all men are capable of understanding simple arguments, though few are capable of complex demonstrations, so in this case it must be sufficient to prove this sense of beauty universal if all men are better pleased with uniformity in the simpler instances than the contrary, even when there is no advantage observed attending it; and likewise if all men, according as their capacity enlarges, so as to receive and compare more complex ideas, have a greater delight in uniformity, and are pleased with its more complex kinds, both original and relative.

Now let us consider if ever any person was void of this sense in the simpler instances. Few trials have been made in the simplest instances of harmony, because as soon as we find an ear incapable of relishing complex compositions, such as our tunes are, no farther pains are employed about such. But in figures, did ever any man make choice of a trapezium, or any irregular curve, for the ichnography or plan of his house, without necessity, or some great motive of [convenience?] [8] Or to make the opposite walls not parallel, or unequal in height? Were ever trapeziums, irregular polygons or curves, chosen for the forms of doors or windows, though these figures might have answered the uses as well, and would have often saved a great part of the time, labour, and expense to workmen which is now employed in suiting the stones and timber to the regular forms? Among all the fantastic modes of dress, none was ever quite void of uniformity, if it were only in the resemblance of the two sides of the same robe, and in some general aptitude to the human form. The pictish painting had always relative beauty, by resemblance to other objects, and often those objects were originally beautiful. However justly we might [here] [9] apply Horace's censure of impertinent descriptions in poetry:

[8] "conveniency" – 1st ed.
[9] Word in brackets added in 3rd ed.

*Sed non erat his locus.*\*10

But never were any so extravagant as to affect such figures as are made by the casual spilling of liquid colours. Who was ever pleased with an inequality of heights in windows of the same range, or dissimilar shapes of them? With unequal legs or arms, eyes or cheeks in a mistress? It must however be acknowledged that interest [may often] 11 counterbalance our sense of beauty in this affair as well as in others, and superior good qualities may make us overlook such imperfections.

*Real beauty alone pleases*

V. Nay farther, it may perhaps appear that regularity and uniformity are so copiously diffused through the universe, and we are so readily determined to pursue this as the foundation of beauty in works of art, that there is scarcely anything ever fancied as beautiful where there is not really something of this uniformity and regularity. We are indeed often mistaken in imagining that there is the greatest possible beauty, where it is but very imperfect; but still it is some degree of beauty which pleases, although there may be higher degrees which we do not observe; and our sense acts with full regularity when we are pleased, although we are kept by a false prejudice from pursuing objects which would please us more.

A Goth, for instance, is mistaken when from education he imagines the architecture of his country to be the most perfect; and a conjunction of [some] 12 hostile ideas may make him have an aversion to Roman buildings, and study to demolish them, as some of our reformers did the popish buildings, not being able to separate the ideas of the superstitious worship from the forms of the buildings where it was practised. And yet it is still real beauty which pleases the Goth, founded upon uniformity amidst variety. For the Gothic pillars are uniform to each other, not only in their sections, which are lozenge-formed, but also in their heights and ornaments. Their arches are not one uniform curve, but yet they are segments of similar curves, and generally equal

---

\* Horace, *De Arte Poetica*, Line 19.
10 "For such things there is a place, but not just now"; trans. H. R. Fairclough.
11 "often may" – 1st ed.
12 "some of the" – 1st ed.

in the same ranges. The very Indian buildings have some kind of uniformity, and many of the Eastern nations, though they differ much from us, yet have great [regularity] [13] in their manner, as well as the Romans in theirs. Our Indian screens, which wonderfully supply [our imaginations] [14] with ideas of deformity, in which nature is very churlish and sparing, do want indeed all the beauty arising from proportion of parts and conformity to nature; and yet they cannot divest themselves of all beauty and uniformity in the separate parts. And this diversifying the human body into various contortions may give some wild pleasure from variety, since some uniformity to the human shape is still retained.

*History pleases in like manner*

VI. There is one sort of beauty which might perhaps have been better mentioned before, but will not be impertinent here, because the taste or relish of it is universal in all nations, and with the young as well as the old, and that is the beauty of history. Everyone knows how dull a study it is to read over a collection of gazettes, which shall perhaps relate all the same events with the historian. The superior pleasure then of history must arise, like that of poetry, from the manners: [when] [15] we see a character well drawn wherein we find the secret causes of a great diversity of seemingly inconsistent actions; or an interest of state laid open, or an artful view nicely unfolded, the execution of which influences very different and opposite actions as the circumstances may alter. Now this reduces the whole to an unity of design at least; and this may be observed in the very fables which entertain children, otherwise we cannot make them relish them.

VII. What has been said will probably be assented to if we always remember in our inquiries into the universality of the sense of beauty that there may be real beauty where there is not the greatest, and that there are an infinity of different forms which may all have some unity, and yet differ from each other. So that men may have different fancies of beauty, and yet uniformity be the universal foundation of our approbation of any form whatsoever as beauti-

[13] "regularity and beauty" – 1st ed.
[14] "the regular imaginations of our ladies" – 1st and 2nd eds.
[15] "as when" – 1st and 2nd eds.

ful. And we shall find that it is so in architecture, gardening, dress, equipage, and furniture of houses, even among the most uncultivated nations, where uniformity still pleases, without any other advantage than the pleasure of the contemplation of it.

*Diversity of judgments concerning our senses*
VIII. It will deserve our consideration on this subject how, in like cases, we form very different judgments concerning the *internal* and *external senses*. Nothing is more ordinary among those, who, after Mr. Locke, have [rejected] [16] *innate ideas,* than to alledge that all our relish for beauty and order is either from [prospect of] [17] advantage, [custom,] [18] or education, for no other reason but the *variety* of fancies in the world; and from this they conclude that our fancies do not arise from any *natural power of perception,* or *sense.* And yet all allow our *external senses* to be *natural,* and that the pleasures or pains of their sensations, however they may be increased or diminished by custom or education, and counterbalanced by interest, yet are really antecedent to custom, habit, education, or prospect of interest. Now it is certain that there is at least as great a variety of fancies about their objects as the objects of beauty. Nay, it is much more difficult, and perhaps impossible, to bring the fancies or relishes of the external senses to any general foundation at all, or to find any rule for the agreeable or disagreeable; and yet we allow that these are *natural* powers of perception.

*The reason of it*
IX. The reason of this different judgment can be no other than this: that we have got distinct names for the external senses, and none, or very few, for the internal, and by this are led, as in many other cases, to look upon the former as some way more fixed and real and natural than the latter. The *sense* of harmony has got its name, viz. a *good ear*; and we are generally brought to acknowledge this *natural* power of *perception,* or *a sense* some way distinct from hearing. Now it is certain that there is as necessary a perception of *beauty* upon the presence of regular objects, as of *harmony* upon hearing certain sounds.

---

[16] "shaken off the groundless opinions about" – 1st and 2nd eds.
[17] Words in brackets added in 2nd ed.
[18] "or custom" – 1st ed.

*An internal sense does not presuppose innate ideas*

X. But let it be observed here once for all that an *internal sense* no more presupposes an *innate idea,* or principle of knowledge, than the *external.* Both are *natural* powers of *perception,* or determinations of the mind to receive necessarily certain ideas from the presence of objects. The *internal sense is a passive power of receiving ideas of beauty from all objects in which there is uniformity amidst variety.* Nor does there seem anything more difficult in this matter than that the mind should be always determined to receive the idea of *sweet* when particles of such a form enter the pores of the tongue, or to have the idea of *sound* upon any quick undulation of the air. The one seems to have as little connection with its idea as the other; and the same power could with equal ease constitute the former the occasion of ideas as the latter.

*Associations cause of disagreements*

XI. The *association of ideas* * above hinted at is one great cause of the apparent diversity of fancies in the sense of beauty, as well as in the external senses, and often makes men have an aversion to objects of beauty, and a liking to others void of it, but under different conceptions than those of beauty or deformity. And here it may not be improper to give some instances of some of these associations. The beauty of trees, their cool shades, and their aptness to conceal from observation have made groves and woods the usual retreat to those who love solitude, especially to the religious, the pensive, the melancholy, and the amorous. And do not we find that we have so joined the ideas of these dispositions of mind with those external objects that they always recur to us along with them? The cunning of the heathen priests might make such obscure places the scene of the fictitious appearances of their deities; and hence we join ideas of something divine to them. We know the like effect in the ideas of our churches, from the perpetual use of them only in religious exercises. The faint light in Gothic buildings has had the same association of a very foreign idea which our poet shows in his epithet,

*A dim religious light.***

* See above, Article III of this Section.
** Milton, *Il Penseroso.*

In like manner it is known that often all the circumstances of actions, or places, or dresses of persons, or voice, or song, which have occurred at any time together, when we were strongly affected by any passion, will be so connected that any one of these will make all the rest recur. And this is often the occasion both of great pleasure and pain, delight and aversion to many objects which of themselves might have been perfectly indifferent to us; but these approbations, or distastes, are remote from the ideas of beauty, being plainly different ideas.

*Music,*
*how it*
*pleases*
*differently*

XII. There is also another charm in music to various persons, which is distinct from harmony and is occasioned by its raising agreeable passions. The human voice is obviously varied by all the stronger passions: now when our ear discerns any resemblance between the air of a tune, whether sung or played upon an instrument, either in its time, or [modulation,] [19] or any other circumstance, to the sound of the human voice in any passion, we shall be touched by it in a very sensible manner, and have melancholy, joy, gravity, thoughtfulness excited in us by a sort of *sympathy* or *contagion*. The same connection is observable between the very air of a tune and the words expressing any passion which we have heard it fitted to, so that they shall both recur to us together, though but one of them affects our senses.

Now in such a diversity of pleasing or displeasing ideas which may be joined with forms of bodies, or tunes, when men are of such different dispositions, and prone to such a variety of passions, it is no wonder that they should often disagree in their fancies of objects, even although their sense of beauty and harmony were perfectly uniform; because many other ideas may either please or displease, according to persons' tempers and past circumstances. We know how agreeable a very wild country may be to any person who has spent the cheerful days of his youth in it, and how disagreeable very beautiful places may be if they were the scenes of his misery. And this may help us in many cases to account for the diversities of fancy, without denying the uniformity of our internal sense of beauty.

[19] "key" – 1st ed.

XIII. *Grandeur* and *Novelty* are two ideas different from *Beauty*, which often recommend objects to us. The reason of this is foreign to the present subject. See *Spectator* No. 412.

## Section VII:

### *Of the Power of Custom, Education, and Example, as to our Internal Senses*

I. Custom, Education, and Example are so often alleged in this affair, as the occasion of our relish for beautiful objects, and for our approbation of, or delight in a certain conduct in life in a moral [species,] [1] that it is necessary to examine these three particularly, to make it appear that there is a natural power of perception, or sense of beauty in objects, antecedent to all custom, education, or example.

*Custom gives no new sense*

II. Custom, as distinct from the other two, operates in this manner. As to actions, it only gives a disposition to the mind or body more easily to perform those actions which have been frequently repeated, but never leads us to apprehend them under any other view than what we were capable of apprehending them under at first, nor gives us any new power of perception about them. We are naturally capable of sentiments of fear, and dread of any powerful presence; and so custom may connect the ideas of religious horror to certain buildings; but [custom could never] [2] have made a being naturally incapable of fear receive such ideas. So had we no other power of perceiving or forming ideas of actions but as they were advantageous or disadvantageous, custom could only have made us more ready at perceiving the advantage or disadvantage of actions. But this is not to our present purpose.

As to our approbation of, or delight in external objects, when the blood or spirits, of which anatomists talk, are roused, quickened, or fermented as they call it, in any agreeable manner by medicine or nutriment, or any glands frequently stimulated to secretion, it is certain that to preserve the body easy, we [shall] [3] delight in objects of taste

---

[1] "sense" – 1st and 2nd eds.
[2] "no custom could" – 1st ed.
[3] "will" – 1st ed.

which of themselves are not immediately pleasant to [it,] [4] if they promote that agreeable state which the body had been accustomed to. Farther, custom will so alter the state of the body that what at first raised uneasy sensations will cease to do so, or perhaps raise another agreeable idea of the same sense. But custom can never give us the idea of a [sense different from those we had] [5] antecedent to it: it will never make the blind approve objects as coloured, or those who have no taste approve meats as delicious, however they [might approve them as] [6] strengthening or exhilarating. Were our glands and the parts about them void of feeling, did we perceive no pleasure from certain brisker motions in the blood, [custom could never] [7] make stimulating or intoxicating fluids or medicines agreeable, when they were not so to the taste. So by like reasoning, had we no natural sense of beauty from uniformity, custom could never have made us imagine any beauty in objects; if we had no ear, custom could never have given us pleasures of harmony. When we have these natural senses antecedently, custom may make us capable of extending our views farther and of receiving more complex ideas of beauty in bodies, or harmony in sounds, by increasing our attention and quickness of perception. But however custom may increase our power of receiving or comparing complex ideas, yet it seems rather to weaken than strengthen the ideas of beauty, or the impressions of pleasure from regular objects, else how is it possible that any person could go into the open air on a sunny day, or clear evening, without the most extravagant raptures, such as Milton * represents our ancestor in upon his first creation? For such any person would fall into upon the first representation of such a scene.

Custom in like manner [may] [8] make it easier for any person to discern the use of a complex machine and approve it as advantageous; but he would never have imagined it beautiful had he no natural sense of beauty. Custom may

[4] "the taste" — 1st ed.
[5] "different sense from what we had" — 1st ed.
[6] "might like such as proved" — 1st ed.
[7] "no custom would" - 1st ed.
* See *Paradise Lost*, Book 8.
[8] "could" — 1st ed.

make us quicker in apprehending the truth of complex theorems, but we all find the pleasure or beauty of theorems as strong at first as ever. Custom makes us more capable of retaining and comparing complex ideas, so as to discern more complicated uniformity which escapes the observation of novices in any art; but all this presupposes a natural sense of beauty in uniformity. For had there been nothing in forms which constituted [the necessary] [9] occasion of pleasure to our senses, no repetition of indifferent ideas as to pleasure or pain, beauty or deformity, could ever have made them grow pleasing or displeasing.

*Nor education* III. The effect of education is this, that thereby we receive many speculative opinions [which are] [10] sometimes true and sometimes false, and are often led to believe that objects may be naturally apt to give pleasure or pain to our external senses [which in reality have] [11] no such qualities. And farther, by education there are some strong associations of ideas without any reason, by mere accident sometimes, as well as by design, which it is very hard for us ever after to break asunder. Thus aversions are raised to darkness, and to many kinds of meat, and to certain innocent actions. Approbations without ground are raised in like manner. But in all these instances, education never makes us apprehend any qualities in objects which we have not naturally senses capable of perceiving. We know what sickness of the stomach is, and may without ground believe that very healthful meats will raise this; we by our sight and smell receive disagreeable ideas of the food of swine, and their styes, and perhaps cannot prevent the recurring of these ideas at table. But never were men naturally blind prejudiced against objects as of a disagreeable colour, or in favour of others as of a beautiful colour. They [perhaps hear] [12] men dispraise one colour, [and may] [13] imagine this colour to be some quite different sensible quality of the other senses, but that is all. And the same way, a man naturally void of taste could by no education receive the ideas of taste, or be prejudiced in

---

[9] "necessarily the" – 1st ed.
[10] Words in brackets added in 2nd ed.
[11] "when in reality the object has" – 1st ed.
[12] "hear perhaps" – 1st ed.
[13] "they" – 1st ed.

favour of meats as delicious. So had we no natural sense of beauty and harmony we [could never] [14] be prejudiced in favour of objects or sounds as beautiful or harmonious. Education may make an unattentive Goth imagine that his countrymen have attained the perfection of architecture, and an aversion to their enemies the Romans may have joined some disagreeable ideas to their very buildings, and excited them to their demolition; but he had never formed these prejudices had he been void of a sense of beauty. Did ever blind men debate whether purple or scarlet were the finer colour, or could any education prejudice them in favour of either as colours?

Thus education and custom may influence our internal senses, where they are antecedently, by enlarging the capacity of our minds to retain and compare the parts of complex compositions; and [then] [15] if the finest objects are presented to us we grow conscious of a pleasure far superior to what common performances excite. But all this presupposes our sense of beauty to be natural. Instruction in anatomy, observation of nature and those airs of the countenance and attitudes of body which accompany any sentiment, action, or passion, may enable us to know where there is a just imitation. But why should an exact imitation please upon observation if we had not naturally a sense of beauty in it, more than the observing the situation of fifty or a hundred pebbles thrown at random? And should we [observe them ever so often, we should] [16] never dream of their growing beautiful.

*Prejudices, how removed*    IV. There is something worth our observation as to the manner of rooting out the prejudices of education, not quite foreign to the present purpose. When the prejudice arises from associations of ideas without any natural connection, we must frequently force ourselves to bear representations of those objects, or the use of them when separated from the disagreeable idea; and this may at last disjoin the unreasonable association, especially if we can join new agreeable ideas to them. Thus opinions of superstition are best removed by pleasant conversation of persons we esteem for

[14] "never could" – 1st ed.
[15] Word in brackets added in 2nd ed.
[16] "repeat our attention to them ever so often, we shall" – 1st ed.

their virtue, or [by observing that they] [17] despise such opinions. But when the prejudice arises from an apprehension or opinion of natural evil as the attendant or consequent of any object or action, if the evil be apprehended to be the constant and immediate attendant, a few trials without receiving any damage will remove the prejudice, as in that against meats. But where the evil is not represented as the perpetual concomitant, but as what may possibly or probably at some time or other accompany the use of the object, there must be frequent reasoning with ourselves, or a long series of trials without any detriment, to remove the prejudice. Such is the case of our fear of spirits in the dark and in church-yards. And when the evil is represented as the consequence perhaps a long time after, or in a future state, it is then hardest of all to remove the prejudice; and this is only to be effected by slow processes of reason, because in this case there can be no trials made. And this is the case of superstitious prejudices against actions apprehended as offensive to the Deity; and hence it is that they are so hard to root out.

*Example not the cause of internal sense*

V. Example seems to operate in this manner. We are conscious that we act very much for pleasure or private good, and [are thereby] [18] led to imagine that others do so too: hence we conclude there must be some perfection in the objects which we see others pursue, and evil in those which we observe them constantly shunning. Or the example of others may serve to us as so many trials to remove the apprehension of evil in objects [to which we had an aversion].[19] But all this is done upon an apprehension of qualities perceivable by the senses which we have; for no example will induce the blind or deaf to pursue objects as coloured or sonorous, nor could example any more engage us to pursue objects as beautiful or harmonious, had we no [natural sense of beauty or harmony.] [20]

Example may make us [conclude without examination] [21] that our countrymen have obtained the perfection of beauty

[17] "seeing them" – 1st ed.
[18] "hence are" – 1st ed.
[19] "which we had an aversion to" – 1st ed.
[20] "sense of beauty or harmony naturally" – 1st ed.
[21] "without examination conclude" – 1st ed.

in their works, or that there is less beauty in the orders of architecture or painting used in other nations, and so content ourselves with very imperfect forms. [And fear of contempt as void of taste or genius often] [22] makes us join in approving the performances of the reputed masters in our country, and restrains those who have naturally a fine genius or the internal sense very acute, from studying to obtain the greatest perfection. It makes also those of a bad taste pretend to [a livelier perception of beauty than in reality they have].[23] But all this presupposes some natural power of receiving ideas of beauty and harmony. Nor can example effect anything farther unless it be to lead men to pursue objects by implicit faith for some perfection which the pursuer is conscious he does not know or which perhaps is some very different quality from the idea perceived by those of a good taste in such affairs.

Section VIII:

*Of the Importance of the Internal Senses in Life,
and the Final Causes of Them*

*Importance of the internal senses*

I. The busy part of mankind may look upon these things as airy dreams of an inflamed imagination which a wise man should despise who rationally pursues more solid possessions independent on fancy; but a little reflection will convince us that the gratifications of our internal senses are as natural, real, and satisfying enjoyments as any sensible pleasure whatsoever, and that they are the chief ends for which we commonly pursue wealth or power. For how is wealth or power advantageous? How do they make us happy, or prove good to us? No otherwise than as they supply gratifications to our senses or faculties of perceiving pleasure. Now, are these senses or faculties only the external ones? No. Everybody sees that a small portion of wealth or power will supply more pleasures of the external senses than we can enjoy. We know that scarcity often heightens these perceptions more than abundance, which cloys the appetite which is

[22] "Often fear of contempt as void of taste or genius" – 1st ed.
[23] "a perception of ideas of beauty when they do not perceive them" – 1st ed.; "a perception of beauty which in reality they have not" – 2nd ed.

necessary to all pleasure in enjoyment; and hence the poet's advice is perfectly just:

*Tu pulmentaria quaere*
*Sudando.*\*1

In short, the only use of a great fortune above a very small one (except in good offices and moral pleasures) must be to supply us with the pleasures of beauty, order, and harmony.

[It is true indeed that (the) [2] noblest pleasures of the internal senses, in the contemplation of the works of nature, (are) [3] exposed to everyone without expense: the poor and the low may have as free use of these objects in this way as the wealthy or powerful. And even in objects which may be appropriated, the property is of little consequence to the enjoyment of their beauty, which is often enjoyed by others beside the proprietor. But then there are other objects of these internal senses which require wealth or power to produce the use of them as frequently as we desire: as appears in architecture, music, gardening, painting, dress, equipage, furniture, of which we cannot have the full enjoyment without property. And there are some confused imaginations which often lead us to pursue property even in objects where it is not necessary to the true enjoyment of them. These are the ultimate motives of our pursuing the greater degrees of wealth, where there are not generous intentions of virtuous actions.] [4]

This is confirmed by the constant practice of the very enemies to these senses. As soon as they think they are got above the world, or extricated from the hurries of avarice and ambition, banished nature will return upon them and set them upon pursuits of beauty and order in their houses, gardens, dress, table, equipage. They are never easy without some degree of this; and were their hearts open to our view, we should see regularity, decency, beauty, as what their wishes terminate upon, either to themselves or their posterity, and what their imagination is always presenting to them

---

\* Horace, *Satires*, Book II, satire ii, Verse 20.
[1] "So earn your sauce with hard exercise"; trans. H. R. Fairclough.
[2] "the enjoyment of the" – 2nd ed.
[3] "is" – 2nd ed.
[4] Passage in brackets added in 2nd ed.

as the possible effects of their labours. Nor without this could they ever justify their pursuits to themselves.

There may perhaps be some instances of human nature perverted into a thorough miser who loves nothing but money, and whose fancy arises no higher than the cold dull thought of possession; but such instances in an age must not be made the standard of mankind against the whole body.

If we examine the pursuits of the luxurious, who [is imagined] [5] wholly devoted to his belly, we shall generally find that the far greater part of his expense is employed to procure other sensations than those of taste, such as fine attendants, regular apartments, services of plate, and the like. Besides, a large share of the preparation must be supposed designed for some sort of generous friendly purposes, to please acquaintance, strangers, parasites. How few would be contented to enjoy the same sensations alone, in a cottage, or out of earthen pitchers? To conclude this point, however these internal sensations may be overlooked in our philosophical inquiries about the human faculties, we shall find in fact that they employ us more and are more efficacious in life, either to our pleasure, or uneasiness, than all our external senses taken together.

*Final causes of the internal senses*

II. As to the *final causes* of this internal sense, we need not inquire whether, to an almighty and all-knowing Being, there be any real excellence in regular forms, in acting by general laws, in knowing by general theorems. We seem scarce capable of answering such questions anyway; nor need we inquire whether other animals may not discern uniformity and regularity in objects which escape our observation, and may not perhaps have their senses constituted so as to perceive beauty from the same foundation which we do, in objects which our senses are not [fit] [6] to examine or compare. We shall confine ourselves to a subject where we have some certain [foundation] [7] to go upon and only inquire if we can find any reasons worthy of the great Author of nature for making such a connection between regular objects and the pleasure which accompanies our perceptions of them; or, what reasons might possibly influence him to

[5] "in the opinion of the world is" – 1st and 2nd eds.
[6] "fitted" – 1st ed.
[7] "foundations – 1st ed.

create the world as it at present is as far as we can observe, everywhere full of regularity and uniformity.

Let it be here observed that as far as we know [concerning] [8] any of the great bodies of the universe, we see forms and motions really beautiful to our senses; and if we were placed in any planet, the apparent courses would still be regular and uniform, and consequently beautiful to [us].[9] Now this gives us no small ground to imagine that if the senses of their inhabitants are in the same manner adapted to their habitations and the objects occurring to their view as ours are here, their senses must be upon the same general foundation with ours.

But to return to the questions, what occurs to resolve them may be contained in the following propositions.

1. The manner of knowledge by universal theorems, and of operation by universal causes, as far as we can attain [it,] [10] must be most convenient for beings of limited understanding and power, since this prevents distraction in their understandings through the multiplicity of propositions, and toil and weariness to their powers of action; and consequently their reason, without any sense of beauty, must approve of such methods when they reflect upon their apparent advantage.

2. Those objects of contemplation in which there is uniformity amidst variety are more distinctly and easily comprehended and retained than irregular objects because the accurate observation of one or two parts often leads to knowledge of the whole. Thus we can from a pillar or two, with an intermediate arch and cornice, form a distinct idea of a whole regular building, if we know of what species it is and have its length and breadth. From a side and solid angle we have the whole regular solid. The measuring one side gives the whole square, one radius the whole [circle,] [11] two diameters an oval, one ordinate and abscissa the parabola. [Thus also other figures, if they have any regularity, are in every point determined from a few data,] [12] whereas it must

[8] "of" – 1st ed.
[9] "our sense" – 1st and 2nd eds.
[10] "to this manner" – 1st ed.
[11] "circle pretty nearly" – 1st ed.
[12] "and so on in more complex figures which have any regularity which can be entirely determined and known in every part from a few data" – 1st and 2nd eds.

be a long attention to a vast multiplicity of parts which can ascertain or fix the idea of any irregular form, or give any distinct idea of it, or make us capable of retaining it, as appears in the forms of rude rocks, and pebbles, and confused heaps, even when the multitude of sensible parts is not so great as in the regular forms; for such irregular objects distract the mind with variety, since for every sensible part we must have a quite different idea.

3. From these two propositions it follows that beings of limited understanding and power, if they act rationally for their own interest, must choose to operate by the simplest means, to invent general theorems, and to study regular objects, if they be [as useful as] [13] irregular ones, that they may avoid the endless toil of producing each effect by a separate operation, of searching [out] [14] each different truth by a different inquiry, and of imprinting the endless variety of dissimilar ideas in irregular objects.

4. But then beside this consideration of interest there does not appear to be any necessary connection, [antecedent] [15] to the constitution of the Author of nature, between [regular] [16] forms, actions, theorems, and that sudden sensible pleasure excited in us upon observation of them, even when we do not reflect upon the advantage mentioned in the former proposition. And so possibly the Deity could have formed us so as to have no [immediate] [17] pleasure from such objects, or connected pleasure from those of a quite contrary nature. We have a tolerable presumption of this in the beauties of various animals; they give some small pleasure indeed to everyone who views them, but then everyone [seems far more delighted with the peculiar beauties of its own species than with those of a different one, which seldom raise any desire.* [18]].[19] This makes it probable that the

[13] "but equal in use with" – 1st ed.
[14] Word in brackets added in 2nd ed.
[15] "antecedently" – 1st ed.
[16] "the regular" – 1st ed.
[17] Word in brackets added in 2nd ed.
* See Cicero, *De Natura Deorum,* Book I, Capital 27.
[18] Footnote added in 4th ed.
[19] "in its own species seems vastly more delighted with their peculiar beauties than with the beauties of a different species which seldom raise any desire but among animals of the same species with the one admired" – 1st ed.; "seems vastly

pleasure is not the necessary result of the form itself, otherwise it would equally affect all apprehensions in what species soever, but depends upon a voluntary constitution adapted to preserve the regularity of the universe, and is probably not the effect of necessity but choice in the Supreme Agent who constituted our senses.

*From the divine goodness*
5. Now from the whole we may conclude that supposing the Deity so kind as to connect sensible pleasure with certain actions or contemplations beside the rational advantage perceivable in them, there is a great moral necessity from his goodness that the internal sense of men should be constituted as it is at present so as to make uniformity amidst variety the occasion of pleasure. For were it not so, but on the contrary, if irregular objects, particular truths and operations pleased us, beside the endless toil this would involve us in, there must arise a perpetual dissatisfaction in all rational agents with themselves, since reason and interest would lead us to simple general causes while a contrary sense of beauty would make us disapprove them. Universal theorems would appear to our understanding the best means of increasing our knowledge of what might be useful, while a contrary sense would set us on the search after particular truths. Thought and reflection would recommend objects with uniformity amidst variety, and yet this perverse instinct would involve us in labyrinths of confusion and dissimilitude. And hence we see how suitable it is to the sagacious bounty which we suppose in the Deity to constitute our internal senses in the manner in which they are, by which pleasure is joined to the contemplation of those objects which a finite mind can best imprint and retain the ideas of with the least distraction; to those actions which are most efficacious and fruitful in useful effect; and to those theorems which most enlarge our minds.

*Reason of general laws*
III. As to the other question, What reason might influence the Deity, whom no diversity of operation could distract or weary, to choose to operate by simplest means and general laws, and to diffuse uniformity, proportion, and similitude through all the parts of nature which we can observe?,

more delighted with the peculiar beauties of its own species than with those of a different one which seldom raise any desire but among animals of the same species with the one admired" – 2nd ed.

perhaps there may be some real excellence in this manner of operation, and in these forms, which we know not. But this we may probably say, that since the divine goodness, for the reasons above mentioned, has constituted our sense of beauty as it is at present, the same goodness might [have determined] [20] the Great Architect to adorn this [stupendous] [21] theatre in [a manner] [22] agreeable to the spectators, and that part which is exposed to the observation of men so as to be pleasant to them, especially if we suppose that he designed to discover himself to them as wise and good, as well as powerful; for thus he has given them greater evidences through the whole earth of his art, wisdom, design, and bounty, than they can possibly have for the reason, counsel, and good-will of their fellow creatures, with whom they converse, with full persuasion of these qualities in them, about their common affairs.

As to the operations of the Deity by general laws, there is [still a farther reason from a sense] [23] superior to these already considered, even that of virtue, or the beauty of action, which is the foundation of our greatest happiness. For were there no general laws fixed to the course of nature, there could be no prudence or design in men, no rational expectation of effects from causes, no schemes of action projected, [or] [24] any regular execution. If, then, according to the frame of our nature, our greatest happiness must depend upon our actions, as [it may perhaps] [25] be made appear it does, the universe must be governed not by particular wills but by general laws upon which we can found our expectations and project our schemes of action. [Nay farther, though general laws did ordinarily obtain, yet if the Deity usually stopped their effects whenever it was necessary to prevent any particular evils, this would effectually and justly supersede all human prudence and care about actions, since a superior mind did thus relieve men from their charge.] [26]

[20] "determine" – 1st and 2nd eds.
[21] "vast" – 1st and 2nd eds.
[22] "that manner which should be" – 1st ed.
[23] "a farther reason from a sense still" – 1st ed.
[24] "nor" – 1st ed.
[25] "perhaps it may" – 1st ed.
[26] Passage in brackets added in 2nd ed.

HUTCHESON'S *REFLECTIONS UPON LAUGHTER*

Francis Hutcheson's *Reflections Upon Laughter* occupies a middle place between his primary philosophical interests: aesthetics and moral theory. It is aesthetic in that it deals with a major category of the fine arts; but it is moral too in that it attempts to establish the social significance of laughter as an instrument of moral criticism.

Hutcheson's point of departure in the *Reflections,* as in his moral treatises, is criticism of Hobbesian egoism. True to form, Hobbes, in *Human Nature* (1650), and *Leviathan* (1651), had found the basis of comedy in a selfish motive. Laughter, he said, was the result either of self-satisfaction or, more importantly, "sudden glory": the sudden realization of your own superiority over someone or something.

Hutcheson apparently takes Hobbes to be stating that sudden glory is the necessary-and-sufficient condition for the comic situation, of which laughter is the sign, and devotes the first of the three papers on laughter to a refutation by counter-example. For if there are comic situations in which there is no feeling of superiority, sudden glory cannot be a necessary condition for comedy; and if there are situations in which there is the feeling of sudden glory but no humor, sudden glory cannot be a sufficient condition for comedy. Thus Hutcheson writes: "If Mr. Hobbes's notion be just, then, first, there can be no laughter on any occasion where we make no comparison of ourselves to others, or of our present state to a worse state, or where we do not observe some superiority of ourselves to others, or of our present state to a worse state, or where we do not observe some superiority of ourselves above some other thing: and again, it must follow, that every sudden appearance of superiority over another must excite laughter, when we attend to it." He argues: "If both these conclusions be false, the notion from whence they are drawn," that is, that sudden glory is a necessary-and-sufficient condition for laughter, "must be so too." [1]

---

[1] Francis Hutcheson, *Reflections Upon Laughter, and Remarks Upon "The Fable of the Bees"* (Glasgow, 1750), p. 7.

The remainder of the first paper is devoted to presenting such counter-examples: instances of comic, laughter-producing situations "without any imagined superiority of ourselves . . . ," [2] and instances of non-comic situations in which "opinion of superiority suddenly incited in us does not move Laughter. . . ." [3] With the producing of these counter-examples, the Hobbesian view that the feeling of sudden glory is a necessary-and-sufficient condition for laughter is defeated, although Hutcheson does not deny that *some* humorous situations are indeed made so in a Hobbesian way, namely, those we call *ridiculous*. Hobbes and his followers, unfortunately, "never distinguished between the words laughter and ridicule: this last is but one particular species of the former, when we are laughing at the follies of others; and in this species there may be some pretence to allege that some imagined superiority may occasion it; but then there are innumerable instances of laughter, where no person is ridiculed; nor does he who laughs compare himself to anything whatsoever." [4]

The second paper on laughter is devoted to an exposition of Hutcheson's own views about the nature of comedy. He takes his cue, here, from Addison (although Addison, as Hutcheson points out in the first paper, agrees with Hobbes's analysis of laughter).

In his influential series of *Spectator* Papers *On the Pleasures of the Imagination* (1712), Addison had distinguished various pleasurable sensations of what we would now call an aesthetic nature, among them those of *beauty, grandeur, novelty*. These are conceived of as in some sense or other "naturally" caused by certain objects and qualities, and not by others, as honey is "naturally" pleasant to the taste and castor oil is "naturally" unpleasant. But by the association of the "naturally" pleasant (say) with some unpleasant event, the "naturally" pleasant might thereby become unpleasant – if, for example, I ate too much honey once as a child and became sick to my stomach, honey might thereafter taste unpleasant to me. So too, a "naturally" unsublime or unbeautiful object might come to excite feelings of sublimity and beauty, or a "naturally" sublime or beautiful object might cease to excite them: "by some strange associations of ideas made in our infancy, we have frequently some of these ideas recurring along with a great many objects, with which they have no other connection than what custom or education, or frequent allusions give them, or at most, some very distant

[2] *Ibid.*
[3] *Ibid.*, p. 11.
[4] *Ibid.*, p. 13.

resemblance." [5] So, for example, "Hail to the Chief" may raise feelings of sublimity in an American because of its association with the "sublime" office of President of the United States, whereas, in fact, it is a rather awkward, trivial, mediocre march, not "naturally" sublime at all.

True literary wit or genius, Addison says in another place, consists in filling the reader's mind with great and sublime ideas and feelings. And this is accomplished most readily by metaphor and simile. As Hutcheson interprets Addison's view, "what we call a great genius, such as becomes a heroic poet, gives us pleasure by filling the mind with great conceptions; and therefore they bring most of their similitudes and metaphors from objects of dignity and grandeur, where the resemblance is generally very obvious." [6]

Now the comic situation arises, according to Hutcheson, by a reversal of the above principle: that is, by the use of *inappropriate* metaphor and simile; by the bringing together of images that are slightly askew but not altogether bizarre. So, to compare Scipio to an eagle is "sublime"; to compare him to an aardvark is just silly; but to compare him to a dodo is neither sublime nor silly, and may be humorous, because a dodo is *something* like an eagle, being a bird, and yet brings along in its wake all kinds of low and mean associations which make the simile laughable rather than sublime. Thus Hutcheson writes: "That then which seems generally the cause of laughter is the bringing together of images which have contrary additional ideas, as well as some resemblance in the principal idea: this contrast between ideas of grandeur, dignity, sanctity, perfection, and ideas of meanness, baseness, profanity, seems to be the very spirit of burlesque; and the greatest part of our railery and jest is founded upon it." [7] We might say, then, in an Aristotelian vein, that the essence of comedy, for Hutcheson, is a mean, in the use of metaphor and simile (and other such devices), between the extremes of the entirely appropriate and the entirely inappropriate. In a certain sense, therefore, the quality of humor, like that of beauty, is based on the notion of unity in variety; but whereas with beauty the emphasis is on the *unity,* with humor it is on the *variety.* The inappropriate comparison, in order to be humor and not merely inappropriate, must bear some affinity to the other term of the simile or metaphor. And therein lies the unity of humor. But that unity must be jarred by the inappropriateness, and therein lies the predominance of variety. Humor, thus, draws on the same principle as the

[5] *Ibid.*, p. 17.
[6] *Ibid.*, p. 18.
[7] *Ibid.*, p. 19.

aesthetic qualities of beauty and harmony. Yet, in a way it is anti-aesthetic.

And while we are on the subject of the relationship between humor and the aesthetic categories of beauty and harmony, it is worth noting that in one very important respect humor stands in marked contrast to these others: it does not seem amenable to a "standard." For humor, as we have seen, is based, to a large degree, on artificial associations of ideas, due to custom and education. The eagle may be "naturally" sublime; but the dodo is foolish and low by custom, and for all that we know may be worshipped as a god in Fiji. "And hence we may see," Hutcheson concludes, "that what is counted ridiculous in one age or nation, may not be so in another." [8] It is true that Hutcheson is not always steady to this text, and at times, in the *Reflections Upon Laughter*, he seems to be passing "objective" value judgments on various kinds of humor. But if this is so, it is an inconsistency. The consequence of relying so heavily on the association of ideas must be *De gustibus non est disputandum.*

Hutcheson concludes the *Reflections Upon Laughter* with a discussion of "the effects of laughter, and the ends for which it was implanted in our nature...." [9] It is here that the aesthetician turns moralist.

The *immediate* effect of laughter is clearly pleasure: "Everyone is conscious that a state of laughter is an easy and agreeable state, that the receiving or suggestion of ludicrous images tends to dispel fretfulness, anxiety, or sorrow, and to reduce the mind to an easy, happy state...." [10] Laughter is the outward sign of a disposition to be pleased (in some special way) by certain situations. And such a disposition must be, in Hutcheson's scheme of things, an "internal sense," like the sense of beauty. Thus Hutcheson takes the notion of a "sense of humor" quite literally. "The implanting then a sense of the ridiculous, in our nature, was giving us an avenue to pleasure, and an easy remedy for discontent and sorrow." [11]

But although the immediate effect of laughter is simple pleasure, its long-term results may involve something more significant. Hutcheson in fact envisions two possible uses of laughter: (1) as a general "socializing" influence; and (2) as a specific against certain moral weaknesses, notably, intellectual fanaticism.

Of the social effects of laughter, Hutcheson has this to say:

[8] *Ibid.*, p. 24.
[9] *Ibid.*, p. 26.
[10] *Ibid.*
[11] *Ibid.*, p. 27.

It is plainly of considerable moment in human society. It is often a great occasion of pleasure, and enlivens our conversation exceedingly, when it is conducted by good-nature. It spreads a pleasantry of temper over a multitude at once; and one merry easy mind may by this means diffuse a like disposition over all who are in company. There is nothing of which we are more communicative than of a good jest. . . .[12]

Laughter, then, is a cohesive element in the social fabric.

In a more specifically moral vein, Hutcheson sees laughter as a palliative for the tendency of men to exaggerate the importance of some idea, or system of ideas, to the extent of erecting false intellectual or even religious idols. It keeps the intellect from becoming inflexible. In a word, Hutcheson conceives of comedy as a weapon against the crank.

It is well known, that our passions of every kind lead us into wild enthusiastic apprehensions of their several objects. When any object seems great in comparison of ourselves, our minds are apt to run into a perfect veneration: when an object appears formidable, a weak mind will run into a pain, an unreasonable, impotent horror. Now in both these cases, by our sense of the ridiculous, we are made capable of relief from any pleasant, ingenious well-wisher, by more effectual means, than the most solemn, sedate reasoning. Nothing is so properly applied to the false grandeur, either of good or evil, as ridicule. . . .[13]

It is always good form to pay tribute to an author's anticipations of future thinkers. And so I will conclude these remarks by suggesting that Hutcheson's notions of the socializing effects of laughter, and its "unstiffening" of the rigid single-minded intellect, bear some affinity to Henri Bergson's more ambitious venture into the philosophy of comedy. In defense of this suggestion I offer the following passage from Bergson's essay on comedy (1900) which the reader may perhaps find anticipated in Hutcheson:

Laughter must be something of this kind, a sort of *social gesture*. By the fear which it inspires, it restrains eccentricity, keeps constantly awake in mutual contact certain activities which might retire into their shell and go to sleep, and in short, softens down whatever the surface of the social body may retain of mechanical inelasticity.[14]

It may be of some interest that Bergson thinks of laughter as a rather ominous threat, whereas Hutcheson thinks of it as the gentle chiding of a good-natured old uncle. But Darwin stands between them; and his world is far more threatening and fearful than Hutcheson's benevolent theodicy, in which the struggle for survival has yet to be heard of.

[12] *Ibid.*, p. 32.
[13] *Ibid.*, pp. 32-33.
[14] Henri Bergson, *Laughter*, ed. Wylie Sypher (Garden City, New York, 1956), p. 73.

# FRANCIS HUTCHESON:

## REFLECTIONS UPON LAUGHTER

### ADVERTISEMENT

The following papers were originally published in the *Dublin Journal* by the late Mr. Arbuckle. Concerning the merit of them, that ingenious author, at the close of his work, expresses himself in the following manner. "The learned and ingenious author of the *Inquiry into the Original of our Ideas of Beauty and Virtue* will therefore, I hope, excuse me if, to do justice to myself, I am obliged to name him for the three papers upon laughter, which are written in so curious and new a strain of thinking: and also for the forty-fifth, forty-sixth, and forty-seventh papers, containing so many judicious remarks on that pernicious book, *The Fable of the Bees.*" [1]

## I
*... Rapias in jus malis ridentem alienis.*
Horace.[2]

### TO HIBERNICUS

There is scarce anything that concerns human nature, which does not deserve to be inquired into. I send you some thoughts upon a very uncommon subject, laughter, which you may publish, if you think they can be of any use, to help us to understand what so often happens in our own minds, and to know the use for which it is designed in the constitution of our nature.

Aristotle, in his *Art of Poetry,* has very justly explained the nature of one species of laughter, viz. the Ridiculing of Persons, the occasion

---

[1] The *Advertisement* was added in the 4th ed. (I am grateful to Anthony Flanders for his bibliographical assistance in preparing the text of the *Reflections*.)

[2] *Sermons,* II.iii.72: "When you drag him into court he will laugh at your expense"; trans. H. R. Fairclough.

or object of which he tells us is: Ἁμάϛτημα τι ϰὶ αἰχϛ ἀνώδυνον ϰὶ οὐ: "some mistake, or some turpitude, without grievous pain, and not very pernicious or destructive." [3] But this he never intended as a general account of all sorts of laughter.

But Mr. Hobbes, who very much owes his character of philosopher to his assuming positive solemn airs, which he uses most when he is going to assert some palpable absurdity, or some ill-natured nonsense, assures us that "Laughter is nothing else but sudden glory, arising from some sudden conception of some eminency in ourselves, by comparison with the infirmity of others, or with our own formerly: for men laugh at the follies of themselves past, when they come suddenly to remembrance, except they bring with them any present dishonour." [4]

This notion the authors of the *Spectators,* No. 47, have adopted from Mr. Hobbes. That bold author having carried on his inquiries, in a singular manner, without regard to authorities, and having fallen into a way of speaking which was much more intelligible than that of the Schoolmen, soon became agreeable to many free wits of his age. His grand view was to deduce all human actions from Self-Love: by some bad fortune he has overlooked everything which is generous or kind in mankind, and represents men in that light in which a thorough knave or coward beholds them, suspecting all friendship, love, or social affection, of hypocrisy, or selfish design or fear.

The learned world has often been told that Puffendorf had strongly imbibed Hobbes's first principles, although he draws much better consequences from them; and this last author, as he is certainly much preferable to the generality of the Schoolmen, in distinct intelligible reasoning, has been made the grand instructor in morals to all who have of late given themselves to that study. Hence it is that the old notions of natural affections, and kind instincts, the *sensus communis,* the *decorum,* and *honestum,* are almost banished out of our books of morals. We must never hear of them in any of our lectures for fear of innate ideas: all must be interest, and some selfish view; laughter itself must be a joy from the same spring.

If Mr. Hobbes's notion be just, then, first, there can be no laughter on any occasion where we make no comparison of ourselves to others, or of our present state to a worse state, or where we do not observe some superiority to ourselves above some other thing: and again, it must follow, that every sudden appearance of superiority over another must

[3] Aristotle, *Poetics,* ch. V.
[4] *Human Nature,* ch. IX. Addison quotes the same passage. Cf. *Leviathan,* Part I, ch. VI.

excite laughter, when we attend to it. If both these conclusions be false, the notion from whence they are drawn must be so too.

First then, that laughter often arises without any imagined superiority of ourselves, may appear from one great fund of pleasantry, the Parody, and Burlesque Allusion, which move laughter in those who may have the highest veneration for the writing alluded to, and also admire the wit of the person who makes the allusion. Thus many a profound admirer of the machinery in Homer and Virgil has laughed heartily at the interposition of Pallas, in *Hudibras,* to save the bold Talgol from the knight's pistol, presented to the outside of his skull:

> But Pallas came in shape of rust,
> And 'twixt the spring and hammer thrust
> Her Gorgon shield, which made the cock
> Stand stiff, as 'twere transform'd to stock.[5]

And few, who read this, imagine themselves superior either to Homer or Butler; we indeed generally imagine ourselves superior in sense to the valorous knight, but not in this point, of firing pistols. And pray, would any mortal have laughed, had the poet told, in a simple unadorned manner, that his knight attempted to shoot Talgol, but his pistol was so rusty that it would not give fire? And yet this would have given us the same ground of sudden glory from our superiority over the doughty knight.

Again, to what do we compare ourselves, or imagine ourselves superior, when we laugh at this fantastical imitation of the poetical imagery, and similitudes of the morning?

> The sun, long since, had in the lap
> Of Thetis taken out his nap;
> And like a lobster boil'd, the morn
> From black to red began to turn.[6]

Many an orthodox Scotch Presbyterian, which sect few accuse of disregard for the holy scriptures, has been put to it to preserve his gravity, upon hearing the application of Scripture made by his countryman Dr. Pitcairn, as he observed a crowd in the streets about a mason, who had fallen along with his scaffold, and was overwhelmed with the ruins of the chimney which he had been building, and which fell immediately after the fall of the poor mason: "Blessed are the dead which die in the

---

[5] *Hudibras,* I, ii, 781.
[6] *Hudibras,* II, ii, 29.

Lord, for they rest from their labours, and their works follow them."
And yet few imagine themselves superior either to the apostle or the
doctor. Their superiority to the poor mason, I am sure, could never have
raised such laughter, for this occurred to them before the doctor's conso-
lation. In this case no opinion of superiority could have occasioned the
laughter, unless we say that people imagined themselves superior to
the doctor in religion: but an imagined superiority to a doctor in religion
is not a matter so rare as to raise sudden joy; and with people who value
religion, the impiety of another is no matter of laughter.

It is said * that when men of wit make us laugh, it is by representing
some oddness or infirmity in themselves, or others. Thus allusions made
on trifling occasions, to the most solemn figured speeches of great
writers, contain such an obvious impropriety, that we imagine ourselves
incapable of such mistakes as the alluder seemingly falls into; so that
in this case too there is an imagined superiority. But in answer to this,
we may observe, that we often laugh at such allusions, when we are
conscious that the person who raises the laugh knows abundantly the
justest propriety of speaking, and knows, at present, the oddness and
impropriety of his own allusion as well as any in company; nay, laughs
at it himself. We often admire his wit in such allusions, and study to
imitate him in it, as far as we can. Now, what sudden sense of glory, or
joy in our superiority, can arise from observing a quality in another,
which we study to imitate, I cannot imagine. I doubt if men compared
themselves with the alluder, whom they study to imitate, they would
rather often grow grave or sorrowful.

Nay, farther, this is so far from truth, that imagined superiority moves
our laughter, that one would imagine from some instances the very
contrary: for if laughter arose from our imagined superiority, then, the
more that any object appeared inferior to us, the greater would be the
jest; and the nearer anyone came to an equality with us, or resemblance
of our actions, the less we should be moved with laughter. But we see,
on the contrary, that some ingenuity in dogs and monkeys, which comes
near to some of our own arts, very often makes us merry; whereas their
duller actions, in which they are much below us, are no matter of jest
at all. Whence the author in the *Spectator* drew his observation, that
the actions of beasts, which move our laughter, bear a resemblance to
a human blunder, I confess I cannot guess; I fear the very contrary is
true, that their imitation of our grave, wise actions would be fittest to
raise mirth in the observer.

* See the *Spectator*.

The second part of the argument, that opinion of superiority suddenly incited in us does not move to laughter, seems the most obvious thing imaginable. If we observe an object in pain while we are at ease, we are in greater danger of weeping than laughing; and yet here is occasion for Hobbes's sudden joy. It must be a very merry state in which a fine gentleman is, when well dressed, in his coach, he passes our streets, where he will see so many ragged beggars, and porters, and chairmen sweating at their labour, on every side of him. It is a great pity that we had not an infirmary or lazar-house to retire to in cloudy weather, to get an afternoon of laughter at these inferior objects: Strange! – that none of our Hobbists banish all canary birds and squirrels, and lap-dogs, and pugs, and cats out of their houses, and substitute in their places asses, and owls, and snails, and oysters, to be merry upon. From these they might have higher joys of superiority, than from those with whom we now please ourselves. Pride, or an high opinion of ourselves, must be entirely inconsistent with gravity; emptiness must always make men solemn in their behaviour; and conscious virtue and great abilities must always be upon the sneer. An orthodox believer, who is very sure that he is in the true way to salvation, must always be merry upon heretics, to whom he is so much superior in his own opinion; and no other passion but mirth should arise upon hearing of their heterodoxy. In general, all men of true sense, and reflection, and integrity, of great capacity for business, and penetration into the tempers and interests of men, must be the merriest little grigs imaginable; Democritus must be the sole leader of all the philosophers; and perpetual laughter must succeed into the place of the long beard,

> ... To be the grace
> Both of our wisdom and our face.[7]

It is pretty strange that the authors whom we mentioned above have never distinguished between the words laughter and ridicule: this last is but one particular species of the former, when we are laughing at the follies of others; and in this species there may be some pretence to allege that some imagined superiority may occasion it. But then there are innumerable instances of laughter where no person is ridiculed; nor does he who laughs compare himself to anything whatsoever. Thus how often do we laugh at some out-of-the-way description of natural objects, to which we never compare our state at all. I fancy few have ever read the City Shower without a strong disposition to laughter, and instead of

[7] *Hudibras*, I, i, 241.

imagining any superiority, are very sensible of a turn of wit in the author which they despair of imitating: thus what relation to our affairs has that simile of *Hudibras,*

> Instead of trumpet and of drum,
> Which makes the warriour's stomach come,
> And whets mens valour sharp, like beer
> By thunder turn'd to vinegar.[8]

The laughter is not here raised against either valour or martial music, but merely by the wild resemblance of a mean event.

And then farther, even in ridicule itself there must be something else than bare opinion to raise it, as may appear from this, that if anyone would relate in the simplest manner these very weaknesses of others, their extravagant passions, their absurd opinions, upon which the man of wit would rally, should we hear the best vouchers of all the facts alleged, we shall not be disposed to laughter by bare narration. Or should one do a real important injury to another, by taking advantage of his weakness, or by some pernicious fraud let us see another's simplicity, this is no matter of laughter: and yet these important cheats do really discover our superiority over the person cheated, more than the trifling impostures of our humourists. The opinion of our superiority may raise a sedate joy in our minds, very different from laughter; but such a thought seldom arises in our minds in the hurry of a cheerful conversation among friends, where there is often an high mutual esteem. But we go to our closets often to spin out some fine conjectures about the principles of our actions, which no mortal is conscious of in himself during the action; thus the same authors above-mentioned tell us that the desire which we have to see tragical representations is because of the secret pleasure we find in thinking ourselves secure from such evils; we know from what sect this notion was derived.

> *Quibus ipse malis liber es, quia cernere suave.*
>                                         Lucretius.[9]

This pleasure must indeed be a secret one, so very secret, that many a kind compassionate heart was never conscious of it, but felt itself in a continual state of horror and sorrow; our desiring such sights flows from a kind instinct of nature, a secret bond between us and our fellow-creatures.

[8] *Hudibras,* I, ii, 107.
[9] *De Rerum Natura,* Book I, line 4: "because to perceive what ills you are free from yourself is pleasant"; trans. W. H. D. Rouse.

*Naturae imperio gemimus cum funus adultae*
*Virginis occurrit, vel terra clauditur infans.*
*... Quis enim bonus ...*
*Ulla aliena sibi credat mala.*

Juvenal.[10]

## II

### TO THE AUTHOR OF THE DUBLIN JOURNAL

*Humano capiti cervicem pictor equinam*
*Jungere si velit, et varias inducere plumas,*
*Undique conlatis membris, ut turpiter atrum*
*Desinat in piscem mulier formosa superne;*
*Spectatum admissi risum teneatis amici?*

Horace.[11]

Sir,

In my former letter, I attempted to show that Mr. Hobbe's account of laughter was not just. I shall now endeavour to discover some other ground of that sensation, action, passion, or affection, I know not which of them a philosopher would call it.

The ingenious Mr. Addison, in his treatise of the pleasures of the imagination, has justly observed many sublimer sensations than those commonly mentioned among philosophers: he observes, particularly, that we receive sensations of pleasure from those objects which are great, new, or beautiful; and, on the contrary, that objects which are more narrow and confined, or deformed and irregular, give us disagreeable ideas. It is unquestionable that we have a great number of perceptions which can scarcely reduce to any of the five senses, as they are commonly explained; such as either the ideas of grandeur, dignity, decency, beauty, harmony; or, on the other hand, of meanness, baseness, indecency, deformity; and that we apply these ideas not only to material objects, but to characters, abilities, actions.

---

[10] *Satires*, XV.138: "It is at Nature's behest that we weep when we meet the bier of a full-grown maiden, or when the earth closes over a babe.... For what good man ... believes that any human woes concern him not?"; trans. G. G. Ramsay.

[11] *De Arte Poetica*, 1: "If a painter chose to join a human head to the neck of a horse, and to spread feathers of many a hue over limbs picked up now here now there, so that what at top is a lovely woman ends below in a black and ugly fish, could you, my friend, if favoured with a private view, refrain from laughing?"; trans. H. R. Fairclough.

It may be farther observed, that by some strange associations of ideas made in our infancy, we have frequently some of these ideas recurring along with a great many objects, with which they have no other connection than what custom and education, or frequent allusions, give them, or at most, some very distant resemblance. The very affections of our minds are ascribed to inanimate objects; and some animals, perfect enough in their own kind, are made constant emblems of some vices or meanness: whereas other kinds are made emblems of the contrary qualities. For instances of these associations, partly from nature, partly from custom, we may take the following ones: sanctity in our churches, magnificence in public buildings, affection between the oak and ivy, the elm and vine; hospitality in a shade, a pleasant sensation of grandeur in the sky, the sea, and mountains, distinct from a bare apprehension or image of their extension; solemnity and horror in shady woods. An ass is the common emblem of stupidity and sloth, a swine of selfish luxury; an eagle of a great genius; a lion of intrepidity; an ant or bee of low industry, and prudent economy. Some inanimate objects have in like manner some accessary ideas of meanness, either for some natural reason, or oftener by mere chance and custom.

Now, the same ingenious author observes, in the *Spectator,* Vol. I, No. 62, that what we call a great genius, such as becomes a heroic poet, gives us pleasure by filling the mind with great conceptions; and therefore they bring most of their similitudes and metaphors from objects of dignity and grandeur, where the resemblance is generally very obvious. This is not usually called wit, but something nobler. What we call grave wit consists in bringing such resembling ideas together, as one could scarce have imagined had so exact a relation to each other; or when the resemblance is carried on through many more particulars than we could have at first expected: and this therefore gives the pleasure of surprise. In this serious wit, though we are not solicitous about the grandeur of the images, we must still beware of bringing in ideas of baseness or deformity, unless we are studying to represent an object as base and deformed. Now this sort of wit is seldom apt to move laughter, more than heroic poetry.

That then which seems generally the cause of laughter is the bringing together of images which have contrary additional ideas, as well as some resemblance in the principal idea: this contrast between ideas of grandeur, dignity, sanctity, perfection, and ideas of meanness, baseness, profanity, seems to be the very spirit of burlesque; and the greatest part of our raillery and jest is founded upon it.

We also find ourselves moved to laughter by an overstraining of wit, by bringing resemblances from subjects of a quite different kind from the subject to which they are compared. When we see, instead of the easiness, and natural resemblance, which constitutes true wit, a forced straining of a likeness, our laughter is apt to arise; as also, when the only resemblance is not in the idea, but in the sound of the words. And this is the matter of laughter in the pun.

Let us see if this thought may not be confirmed in many instances. If any writing has obtained an high character for grandeur, sanctity, inspiration, or sublimity of thoughts, and boldness of images, the application of any known sentence of such writings to low, vulgar, or base subjects, never fails to divert the audience, and set them a laughing. This fund of laughter the ancients had by allusions to Homer: of this the lives of some of the philosophers in Diogenes Laertius supply abundance of instances. Our late burlesque writers derive a great part of their pleasantry from their introducing, on the most trifling occasions, allusions to some of the bold schemes, or figures, or sentences, of the great poets, upon the most solemn subjects. *Hudibras* and *Don Quixote* will supply one with instances of this in almost every page. It were to be wished that the boldness of our age had never carried their ludicrous allusions to yet more venerable writings. We know that allusions to the phrases of holy writ have obtained to some gentlemen a character of wit, and often furnish laughter to their hearers, when their imaginations have been too barren to give any other entertainment. But I appeal to the religious themselves, if these allusions are not apt to move laughter, unless a more strong affection of the mind, a religious horror at the profanity of such allusions, prevents their allowing themselves the liberty of laughing at them. Now in this affair I fancy anyone will acknowledge that an opinion of superiority is not at all the occasion of the laughter.

Again, any little accident to which we have joined the idea of meanness, befalling a person of great gravity, ability, dignity, is a matter of laughter, for the very same reason; thus the strange contortions of the body in a fall, the dirtying of a decent dress, the natural functions which we study to conceal from sight, are matter of laughter when they occur to observation in persons of whom we have high ideas. Nay, the very human form has the ideas of dignity so generally joined with it, that even in ordinary persons such mean accidents are matter of jest; but still the jest is increased by the dignity, gravity, or modesty of the person, which shows that it is this contrast, or opposition of ideas of dignity and meannness, which is the occasion of laughter.

We generally imagine in mankind some degree of wisdom above other animals, and have high ideas of them on this account. If then along with our notion of wisdom in our fellows, there occurs any instance of gross inadvertence, or great mistake, this is a great cause of laughter. Our countrymen are very subject to little trips of this kind, and furnish often some diversion to their neighbours, not only by mistakes in their speech, but in actions. Yet even this kind of laughter cannot well be said to arise from our sense of superiority. This alone may give a sedate joy, but not be a matter of laughter, since we shall find the same kind of laughter arising in us, where this opinion of superiority does not attend it: for if the most ingenious person in the world, whom the whole company esteems, should through inadvertent hearing, or any other mistake, answer quite from the purpose, the whole audience may laugh heartily, without the least abatement of their good opinion. Thus we know some very ingenious men have not in the least suffered in their characters by an extemporary pun, which raises the laugh very readily; whereas a premeditated pun, which diminishes our opinion of a writer, will seldom raise any laughter.

Again, the more violent passions, as fear, anger, sorrow, compassion, are generally looked upon as something great and solemn; the beholding of these passions in another strikes a man with gravity. Now if these passions are artfully, or accidentally, raised upon a small or fictitious occasion, they move the laughter of those who imagine the occasions to be small and contemptible, or who are conscious of the fraud: this is the occasion of the laugh in biting, as they call such deceptions.

According to this scheme, there must necessarily arise a great diversity in men's sentiments of the ridiculous in actions or characters, according as their ideas of dignity and wisdom are various. A truly wise man, who places the dignity of human nature in good affections and suitable actions, may be apt to laugh at those who employ their most solemn and strong affections about what, to the wise man, appears perhaps very useless or mean. The same solemnity of behaviour and keenness of passion, about a place or ceremony, which ordinary people only employ about the absolute necessaries of life, may make them laugh at their betters. When a gentleman of pleasure, who thinks that good fellowship and gallantry are the only valuable enjoyments of life, observes men, with great solemnity and earnestness, heaping up money, without using it, or incumbering themselves with purchases and mortages, which the gay gentleman, with his paternal revenues, thinks very silly affairs, he may make himself very merry upon them: and the frugal man, in his turn, makes the same jest of the man of pleasure. The successful gamester, whom no disaster forces to lay aside the trifling ideas of an amusement in his play, may laugh to see the serious looks and passions of the gravest business arising in the loser, amidst the ideas of a recreation. There is indeed in these last cases an opinion of superiority in the laughter; but this is not the proper occasion of his laughter; otherwise I see not how we should ever meet with a composed countenance anywhere. Men have their different relishes of life, most people prefer their own taste to that of others; but this moves no laughter, unless, in representing the pursuits of others, they do join together some whimsical image of the opposite ideas.

In the more polite nations, there are certain modes of dress, behaviour, ceremony, generally received by all the better sort, as they are commonly called: to these modes, ideas of decency, grandeur, and dignity are generally joined. Hence men are fond of imitating the mode; and if in any polite assembly, a contrary dress, behaviour, or ceremony appear, to which we have joined in our country the contrary ideas of meanness, rusticity, sullenness, a laugh does ordinarily arise, or a disposition to it, in those who have not the thorough good breeding, or reflection, to restrain themselves, or break through these customary associations.

And hence we may see, that what is counted ridiculous in one age or nation, may not be so in another. We are apt to laugh at Homer, when he compares Ajax unwillingly retreating to an ass driven out of a cornfield; or when he compares him to a boar; or Ulysses tossing all night without sleep through anxiety to a pudding frying on the coals. Those three similes have got low mean ideas joined to them with us, which it is very probable they had not in Greece in Homer's days; nay, as to one of them, the boar, it is well known that in some countries of Europe, where they have wild boars for hunting, even in our times, they have not these low sordid ideas joined to that animal, which we have in these kingdoms, who never see them but in their dirty styes, or on dunghills. This may teach us how impermanent a great many jests are, which are made upon the style of some other ancient writings, in ages when manners were very different from ours, though perhaps fully as rational, and every way as human and just.

## III

*. . . Ridiculum acri*
*Fortius et melius magnas plerumque secat res.*[12]

Sir,

To treat this subject of laughter gravely may subject the author to a censure like to that which Longinus makes upon a prior treatise of the Sublime, because wrote in a manner very unsuitable to the subject. But yet it may be worth our pains to consider the effects of laughter, and the ends for which it was implanted in our nature, that thence we may know the proper use of it: which may be done in the following observations.

First, we may observe, that laughter, like many other dispositions of our mind, is necessarily pleasant to us, when it begins in the natural manner, from one perception in the mind of something ludicrous, and does not take its rise unnaturally from external motions in the body. Everyone is conscious that a state of laughter is an easy and agreeable state, that the recurring or suggestion of ludicrous images tends to dispel fretfulness, anxiety, or sorrow, and to reduce the mind to an easy, happy state; as on the other hand, an easy and happy state is that in which we are most lively and acute in perceiving the ludicrous in objects. Anything that gives us pleasure puts us also in a fitness for laughter, when something ridiculous occurs; and ridiculous objects, occurring to a soured temper, will be apt to recover it to easiness. The implanting then a sense of the ridiculous, in our nature, was giving us an avenue to pleasure, and an easy remedy for discontent and sorrow.

Again, laughter, like other associations, is very contagious: our whole frame is so sociable, that one merry countenance may diffuse cheerfulness to many; nor are they all fools who are apt to laugh before they know the jest, however curiosity in wise men may restrain it, that their attention may be kept awake.

We are disposed by laughter to a good opinion of the person who raises it, if neither ourselves nor our friends are made the butt. Laughter is none of the smallest bonds to common friendships, though it be of less consequence in great heroic friendships.

---

[12] Horace, *Satires*, I.x.14-15: "Jesting oft cuts hard knots more forcefully and effectively than gravity"; trans. H. R. Fairclough. I am most grateful to Michael Hanifin and Margit Minkin of Rutgers University for identifying this quotation.

If an object, action, or event, be truly great in every respect, it will have no natural relation or resemblance to anything mean or base; and consequently no mean idea can be joined to it with any natural resemblance. If we make some forced remote jests upon such subjects, they can never be pleasing to a man of sense and reflection, but raise contempt of the ridiculer, as void of just sense of those things which are truly great. As to any great and truly sublime sentiments, we may perhaps find that, by a playing upon words, they may be applied to a trifling or mean action, or object; but this application will not diminish our high idea of the great sentiment. He must be of a poor trifling temper who would lose his relish of the grandeur and beauty of that noble sentence of the holy writ, mentioned in the former paper, from the doctor's application of it. *Virgil Travesty* [13] may often come into an ingenious man's head, when he reads the original, and make him uneasy with impertinent interruptions, but will never diminish his admiration of Virgil. Who dislikes that line in Homer, by which Diogenes the Cynic answered his neighbour at an execution, who was inquiring into the cause of the criminal's damnation, which had been the counterfeiting of the ancient purple?

Ἔλλαβε ποςφύςεϑ Οαναϑ ῳ μοῖεα χεαταιπ. [14]

Let any of our wits try their mettle in ridiculing the opinion of a good and wise mind governing the whole universe; let them try to ridicule integrity and honesty, gratitude, generosity, or the love of one's country, accompanied with wisdom. All their art will never diminish the admiration which we must have for such dispositions, wherever we observe them pure and unmixed with any low views, or any folly in the exercise of them.

When in any object there is a mixture of what is truly great, along with something weak or mean, ridicule may, with a weak mind which cannot separate the great from the mean, bring the whole into disesteem, or make the whole appear weak or contemptible: but with a person of just discernment and reflection it will have no other effect but to separate what is great from what is not so.

When any object either good or evil is aggravated and increased by the violence of our passions, or an enthusiastic admiration, or fear, the

---

[13] Paul Scarron, *Le virgile traveste*.

[14] Homer, *Iliad*, V.83: "and down over his eyes came dark death and mighty fate"; trans. A. T. Murray. The story about Diogenes the Cynic is told in Diogenes Laertius, *Lives of the Philosophers*, VI.57. According to Diogenes Laertius, the man had stolen the purple, not counterfeited it. The point of the line is that the word which meant "dark" in Homeric Greek later came to mean "purple." (I am most grateful to Michael Rohr of Rutgers University for identifying the quotation and providing the other information in this note.)

application of ridicule is the readiest way to bring down our high imaginations to a conformity to the real moment or importance of the affair. Ridicule gives our minds as it were a bend to the contrary side; so that upon reflection they may be more capable of settling in a just conformity to nature.

Laughter is received in a different manner by the person ridiculed, according as he who uses the ridicule evidences good-nature, friendship, and esteem of the person whom he laughs at, or the contrary.

The enormous crime or grievous calamity of another is not itself a subject which can be naturally turned into ridicule: the former raises horror in us, and hatred, and the latter pity. When laughter arises on such occasions, it is not excited by the guilt or the misery. To observe the contortions of the human body in the air, upon the blowing up of an enemy's ship, may raise laughter in those who do not reflect on the agony and distress of the sufferers; but the reflecting on this distress could never move laughter of itself. So some fantastic circumstances accompanying a crime may raise laughter; but a piece of cruel barbarity, or treacherous villany, of itself, must raise very contrary passions. A jest is not ordinary in an impeachment of a criminal, or an investive oration: it rather diminishes than increases the abhorrence in the audience, and may justly raise contempt of the orator for an unnatural affectation of wit. Jesting is still more unnatural in discourses designed to move compassion toward the distressed. A forced unnatural ridicule, on either of these occasions, must be apt to raise, in the guilty or the miserable, hatred against the laughter; since it must be supposed to show from hatred in him toward the object of his ridicule, or from want of all compassion. The guilty will take laughter to be a triumph over him as contemptible; the miserable will interpret it as hardness of heart, and insensibility of the calamities of another. This is the natural effect of joining to either of these objects mean ludicrous ideas.

If smaller faults, such as are not inconsistent with a character in the main amiable, be set in a ridiculous light, the guilty are apt to be made sensible of their folly, more than by a bare grave admonition. In many of our faults, occasioned by too great violence of some passion, we get such enthusiastic apprehensions of some objects, as lead us to justify our conduct: the joining of opposite ideas or images allays this enthusiasm; and, if this be done with good nature, it may be the least offensive, and most effectual, reproof.

Ridicule upon the smallest faults, when it does not appear to flow from kindness, is apt to be extremely provoking, since the applying of mean ideas to our conduct discovers contempt of us in the ridiculer, and that he designs to make us contemptible to others.

Ridicule applied to those qualities or circumstances in one of our companions, which neither he nor the ridiculer thinks dishonourable, is agreeable to everyone; the butt himself is as well pleased as any in company.

Ridicule upon any small misfortune or injury, which we have received with sorrow or keen resentment, when it is applied by a third person, with appearance of good-nature, is exceeding useful to abate our concern or resentment, and to reconcile us to the person who injured us, if he does not persist in his injury.

From this consideration of the effects of laughter it may be easy to see for what cause, or end, a sense of the ridiculous was implanted in human nature, and how it ought to be managed.

It is plainly of considerable moment in human society. It is often a great occasion of pleasure, and enlivens our conversation exceedingly, when it is conducted by good-nature. It spreads a pleasantry of temper over multitudes at once; and one merry easy mind may by this means diffuse a like disposition over all who are in company. There is nothing of which we are more communicative than of a good jest: and many a man, who is incapable of obliging us otherwise, can oblige us by his mirth, and really insinuate himself into our kind affections, and good wishes.

But this is not all the use of laughter. It is well-known that our passions of every kind lead us into wild enthusiastic apprehensions of their several objects. When any object seems great in comparison of ourselves, our minds are apt to run into a perfect veneration: when an object appears formidable, a weak mind will run into a panic, an unreasonable, impotent horror. Now in both these cases, by our sense of the ridiculous, we are made capable of relief from any pleasant, ingenious well-wisher, by more effectual means, than the most solemn, sedate reasoning. Nothing is so properly applied to the false grandeur, either of good or evil, as ridicule: nothing will sooner prevent our excessive admiration of mixed grandeur, or hinder our being led by that, which is, perhaps, really great in such an object, to imitate also and approve what is really mean.

I question not but the jest of Elijah upon the false deity, whom his countrymen had set up, had been very effectual to rectify their notions of the divine nature, as we find that like jests have been very seasonable in other nations. Baal, no doubt, had been represented as a great personage of unconquerable power; but how ridiculous does the image appear, when the prophet sets before them, at once, the poor ideas which must arise from such a limitation of nature as could be represented by their statues, and the high ideas of omniscience, and omnipotence, with which the people declared themselves possessed by their invocation: "Cry aloud, either he is talking, or pursuing, or he is on a journey, or he is asleep."

This engine of ridicule, no doubt, may be abused, and have a bad effect upon a weak mind; but with men of any reflection, there is little fear that it will ever be very pernicious. An attempt of ridicule before such men, upon a subject every way great, is sure to return upon the author of it. One might dare the boldest wit in company with men of sense, to make a jest upon a completely great action, or character. Let him try the story of Scipio and his fair captive, upon the taking of Cartagena, or the old story of Pylades and Orestes; I fancy he would sooner appear in a fool's coat himself, than he could put either of these characters in such a dress. The only danger is in objects of a mixed nature before people of little judgment, who, by jests upon the weak side, are sometimes led into neglect, or contempt, of that which is truly valuable in any character, institution, or office. And this may show us the impertinence, and pernicious tendency of general undistinguished jests upon any character, or office, which has been too much over-rated. But, that ridicule may be abused, does not prove it useless, or unnecessary, more than a like possibility of abuse would prove all our senses and passions impertinent or hurtful. Ridicule, like other edged tools, may do good in a wise man's hands, though fools may cut their fingers with it, or be injurious to an unwary bystander.

The rules to avoid abuse of this kind of ridicule are, first, either never to attempt ridicule upon what is every way great, whether it be any great being, character, or sentiments; or, if our wit must sometimes run into allusions, on low occasions, to the expressions of great sentiments, let it not be in weak company, who have not a just discernment of true grandeur. And, secondly, concerning objects of a mixed nature, partly great, and partly mean, let us never turn the meanness into ridicule without acknowledging what is truly great, and paying a just veneration to it. In this sort of jesting we ought to be cautious of our company.

> *Discit enim citius, meminitque libentius illud,*
> *Quod quis deridet, quam quod probat et veneratur.*
>
> Horace.[15]

Another valuable purpose of ridicule is with relation to smaller vices, which are often more effectually corrected by ridicule, than by grave

[15] *Epistles*, II.i.262: "For men more quickly learn and more gladly recall what they deride than what they approve and esteem"; trans. H. R. Fairclough.

admonition. Men have been laughed out of faults which a sermon could not reform; nay, there are many little indecencies which are improper to be mentioned in such solemn discourses. Now ridicule, with contempt or ill-nature, is indeed always irritating and offensive; but we may, by testifying a just esteem for the good qualities of the person ridiculed, and our concern for his interests, let him see that our ridicule of his weakness flows from love to him, and then we may hope for a good effect. This then is another necessary rule, that along with our ridicule of smaller faults we should always join evidences of good-nature and esteem.

As to jests upon imperfections, which one cannot amend, I cannot see of what use they can be: men of sense cannot relish such jests; foolish trifling minds may by them be led to despise the truest merit, which is not exempted from the casual misfortunes of our moral state. If these imperfections occur along with a vicious character, against which people should be alarmed and cautioned, it is below a wise man to raise aversions to bad men from their necessary infirmities, when they have a juster handle from their vicious dispositions.

I shall conclude this essay with the words of father Malebranche, upon the last subject of laughter, the smaller misfortunes of others. That author amidst all his visions shows sometimes as fine sense as any of his neighbours.

"*There is nothing more admirably contrived than those natural correspondences observable between the inclinations of men's minds and the motions of their bodies. . . . All this secret chain-work is a miracle, which can never sufficiently be admired or understood. Upon sense of some surprising evil, which appears too strong for one to overcome with his own strength, he raises, suppose, a loud cry: this cry, forced out by the disposition of our machine, pierces the ears of those who are near, and makes them understand it, let them be of what nation or quality soever; for it is the cry of all nations, and all conditions, as indeed it ought to be. It raises a commotion in their brain, . . . and makes them run to give succour without so much as knowing it. It soon obliges their will to desire, and their understanding to contrive, provided that it was just and according to the rules of society. For an indiscreet cry-out, made upon no occasion, or out of an idle fear, produces, in the assistants, indignation or laughter instead of pity. . . . That indiscreet cry naturally produces aversion, and desire of revenging the affront offered to nature, if he that made it without cause, did it wilfully: but it ought

_____

* Book IV, chapter 13.

only to produce the passion of derision, mingled with some compassion, without aversion or desire of revenge, if it were a fright, that is, a false appearance of a pressing exigency which caused the clamour. For scoff or ridicule is necessary to reassure and correct the man as fearful; and compassion to succour him as weak. It is impossible to conceive anything better ordered." [16]

I am, Sir,

Your very humble servant,

Philomeides.

---

[16] Nicolas Malebranche, *De la recherche de la vérité*. The passage is quoted, with a few inaccuracies, from the English translation of T. Taylor (London, 1700), p. 166.

# INDEX